Name: ________________

Learn to write letters and numbers

Children's workbook from 3 to 6:
Prepare children for success in school with a
handwriting-learning book that teaches
children to write letters, numbers, animal
names and types and more to enhance their
skills and minds in reading, writing and
learning about animals. Discover the guide to
learning to write on your own, really fun.

Learn to handwriting
Aa Bb Cc Dd Ee Ff Gg
Hh Ii Jj Kk Ll Mm
Nn Oo Pp
Qq Rr Ss Tt Uu Vv Ww Xx Yy Zz
ZOO
ALPHABET
1 2 3 4 5 6 7 8 9 0

Alligator

Name: ______________

A a

A A

a a

apple

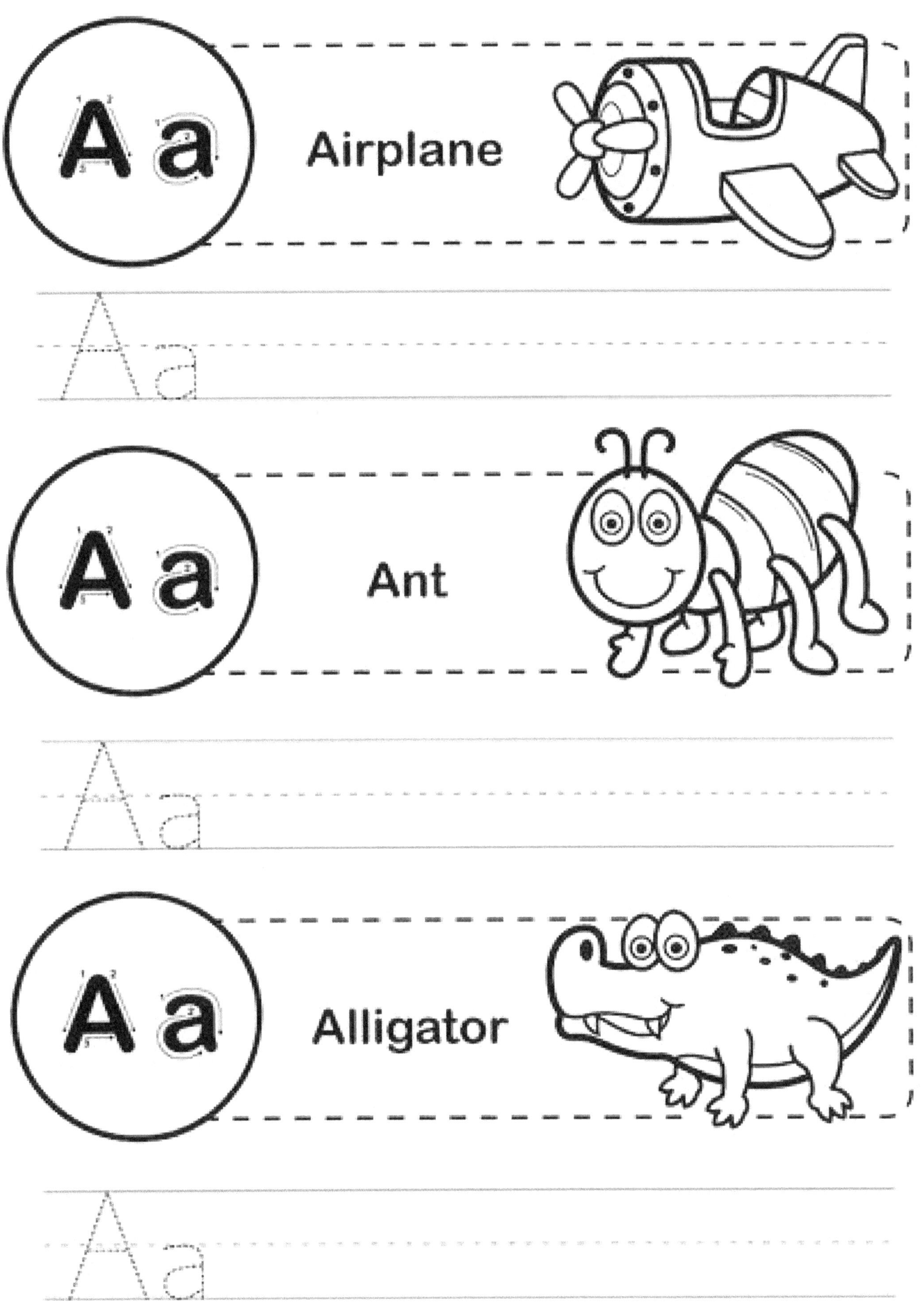

A a
Airplane
A a
Ant
A a
Alligator

Bear

B B

b b

bee

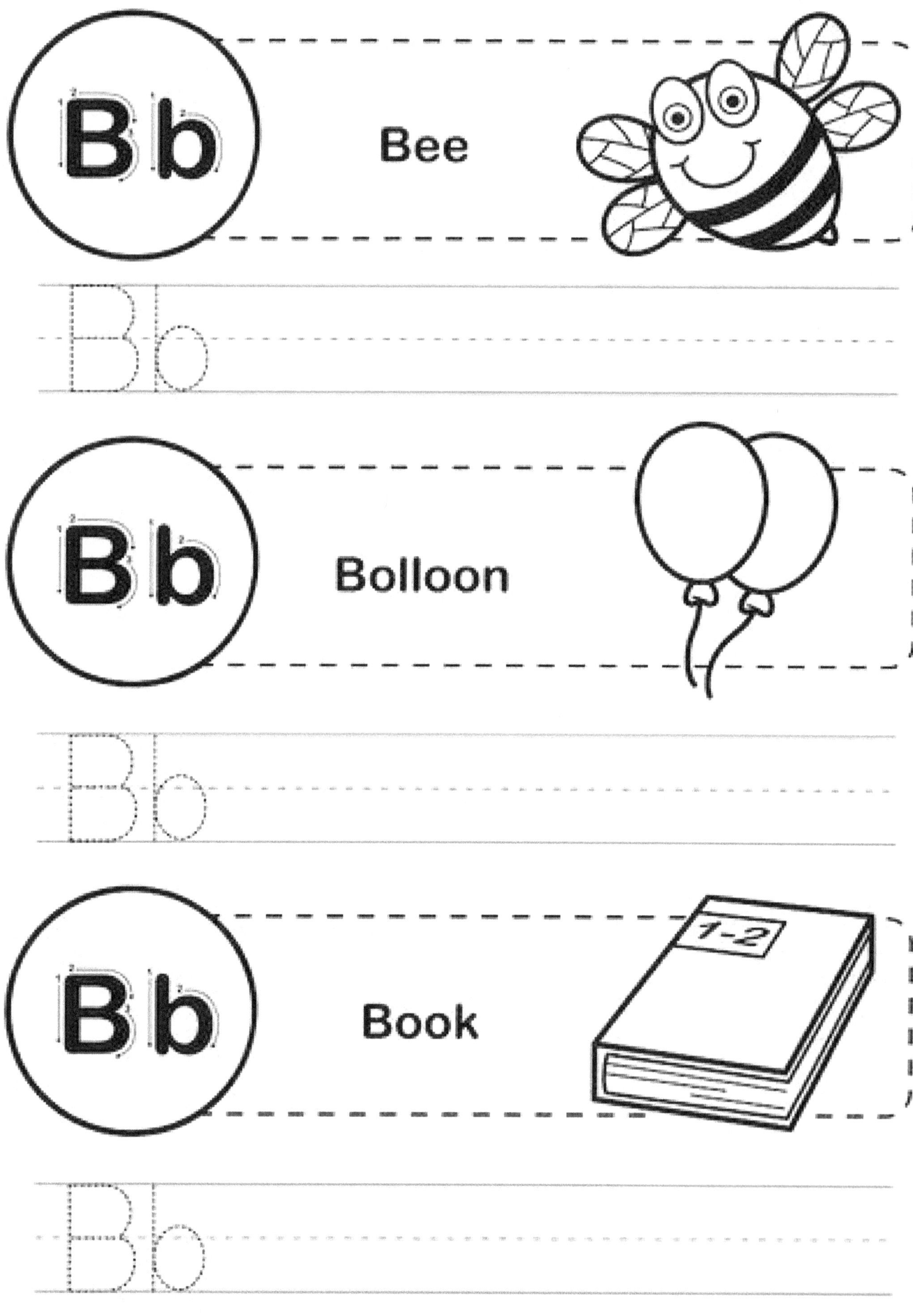

B b

Bee

B b

B b

Bolloon

B b

B b

Book

B b

Cow

C c

C c

c c

cat

C c
Cap
C c
Candle
C c
Cake

Deer

Name: _______________

D d

D

d

dog

D d
Door
D d
Dinosaur
D d
Dragon Fruit

Elephant

Name: _______________________

E

e

elephant

E e
Elephant

E e
Egg

E e
Earth

Fox

Name: _______________________

F f
Flower
F f
Frog
F f
Fork

Giraffe

G G

g g

giraffe

G g

Gift

G g

Goat

G g

Grape

Hedgehog

H

h

hen

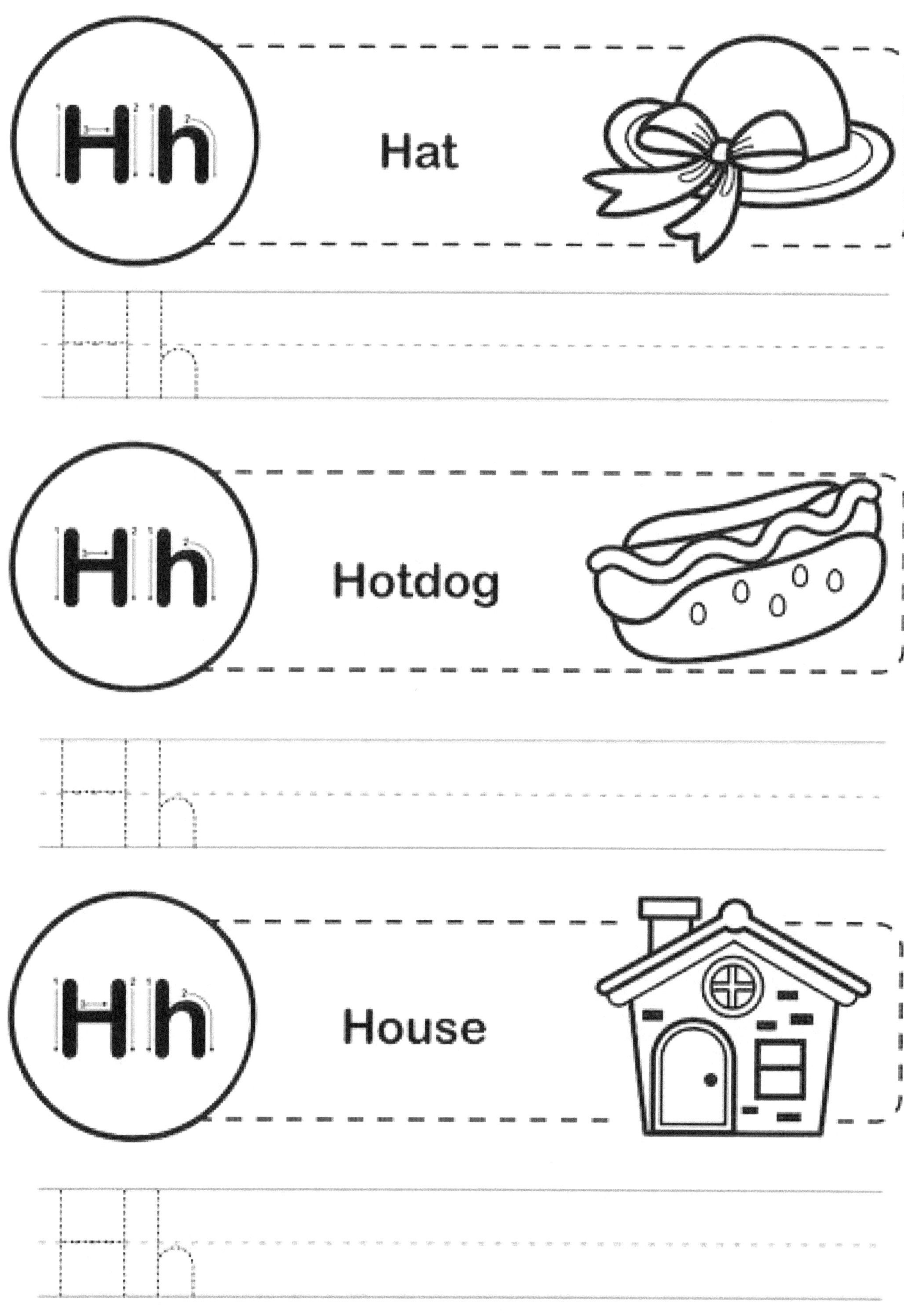

H h
Hat
H h
Hotdog
H h
House

Iguana

I

i

ink

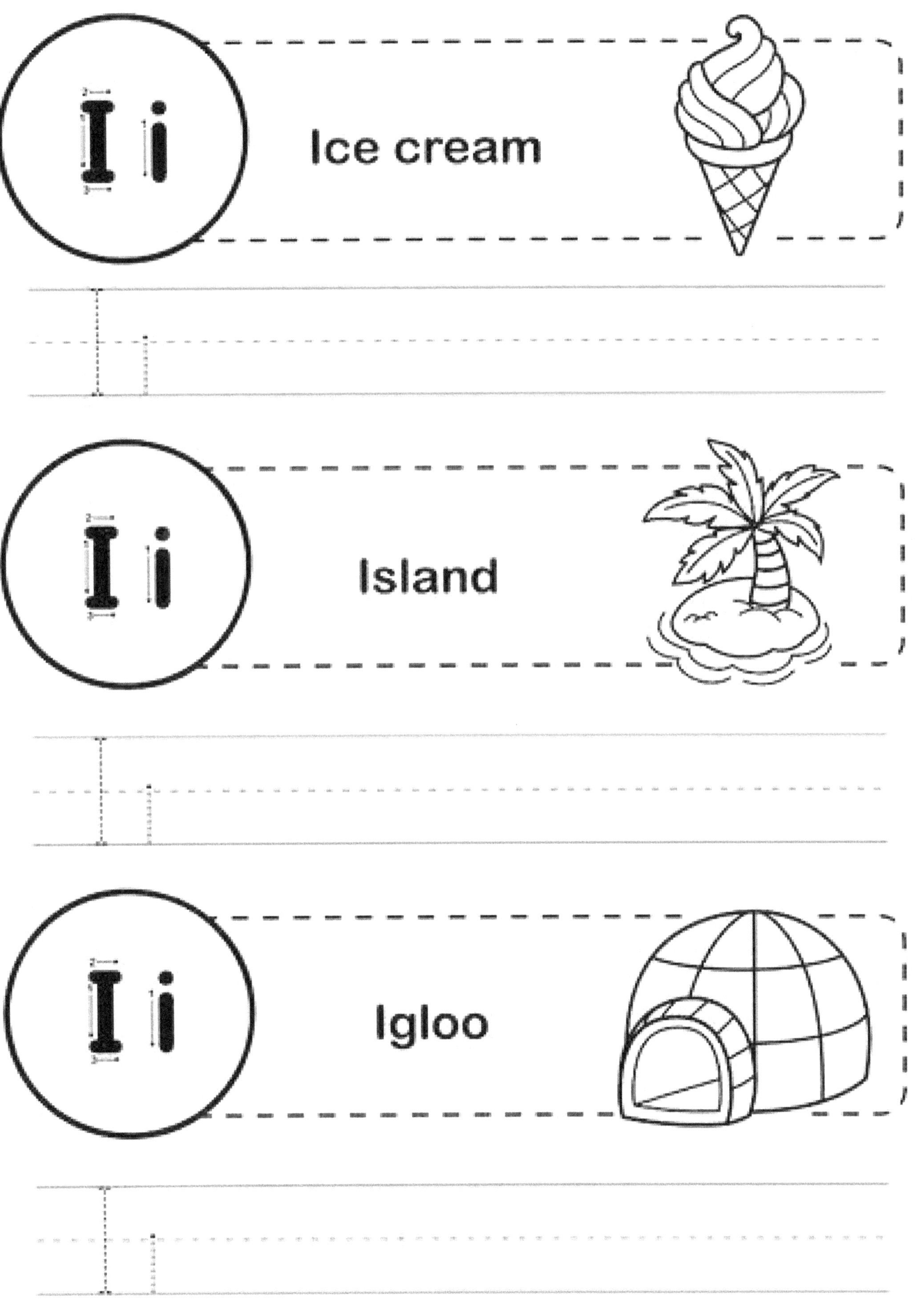

I i
Ice cream
I i
Island
I i
Igloo

Jellyfish

J

j

jellyfish

J j
Jam
J j
Juice
J j
Joker

Kangaroo

Name: _______________

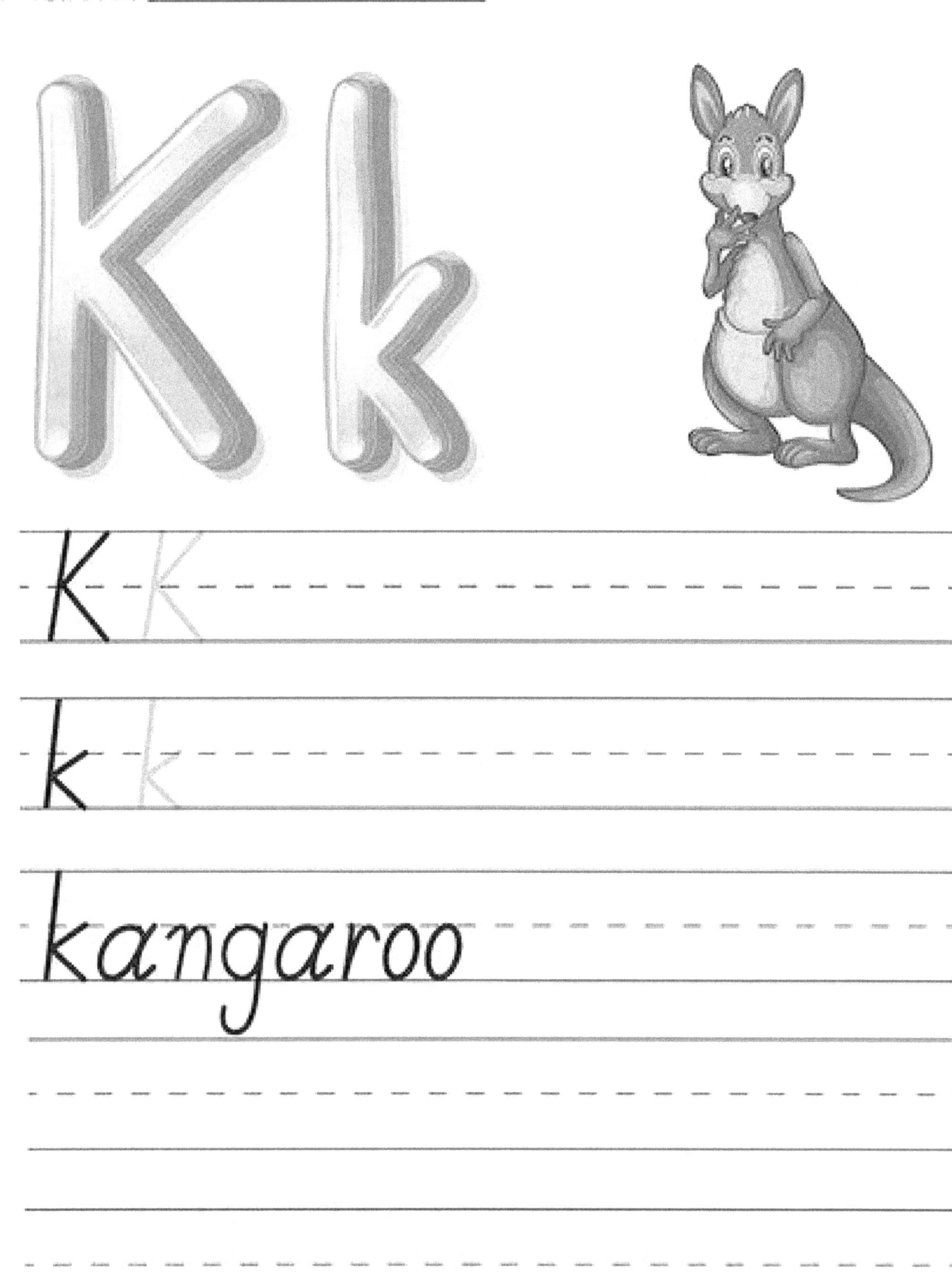

K k
K
k
kangaroo

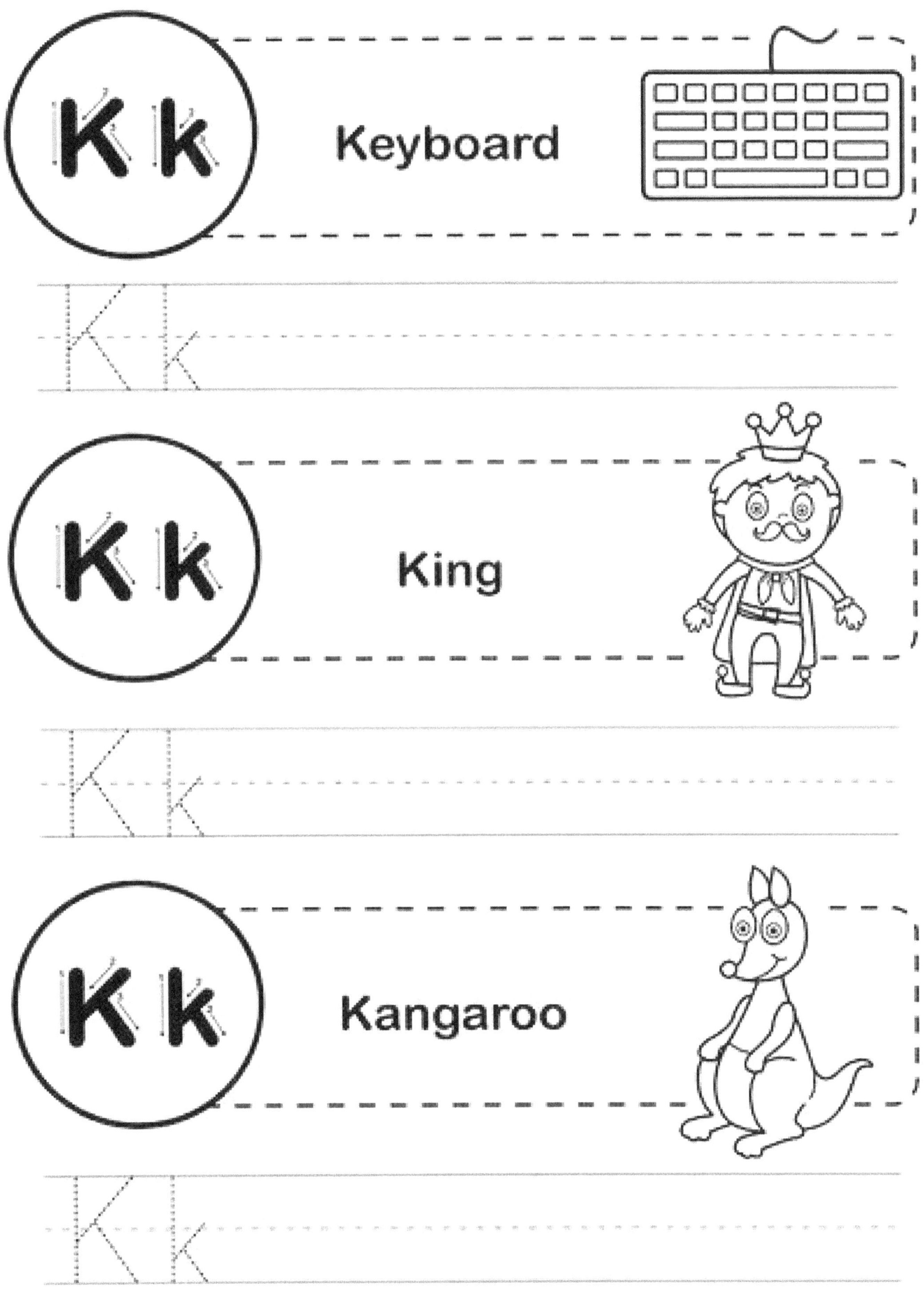

Keyboard

King

Kangaroo

Lion

lion

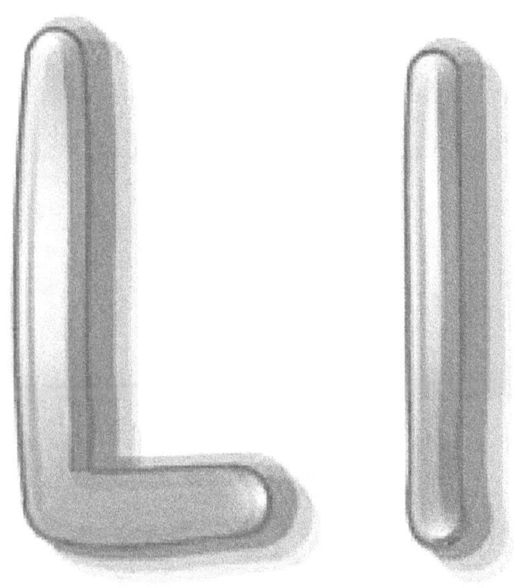

L

l

lion

Lamp
Ladybug
Leaves

Monkey

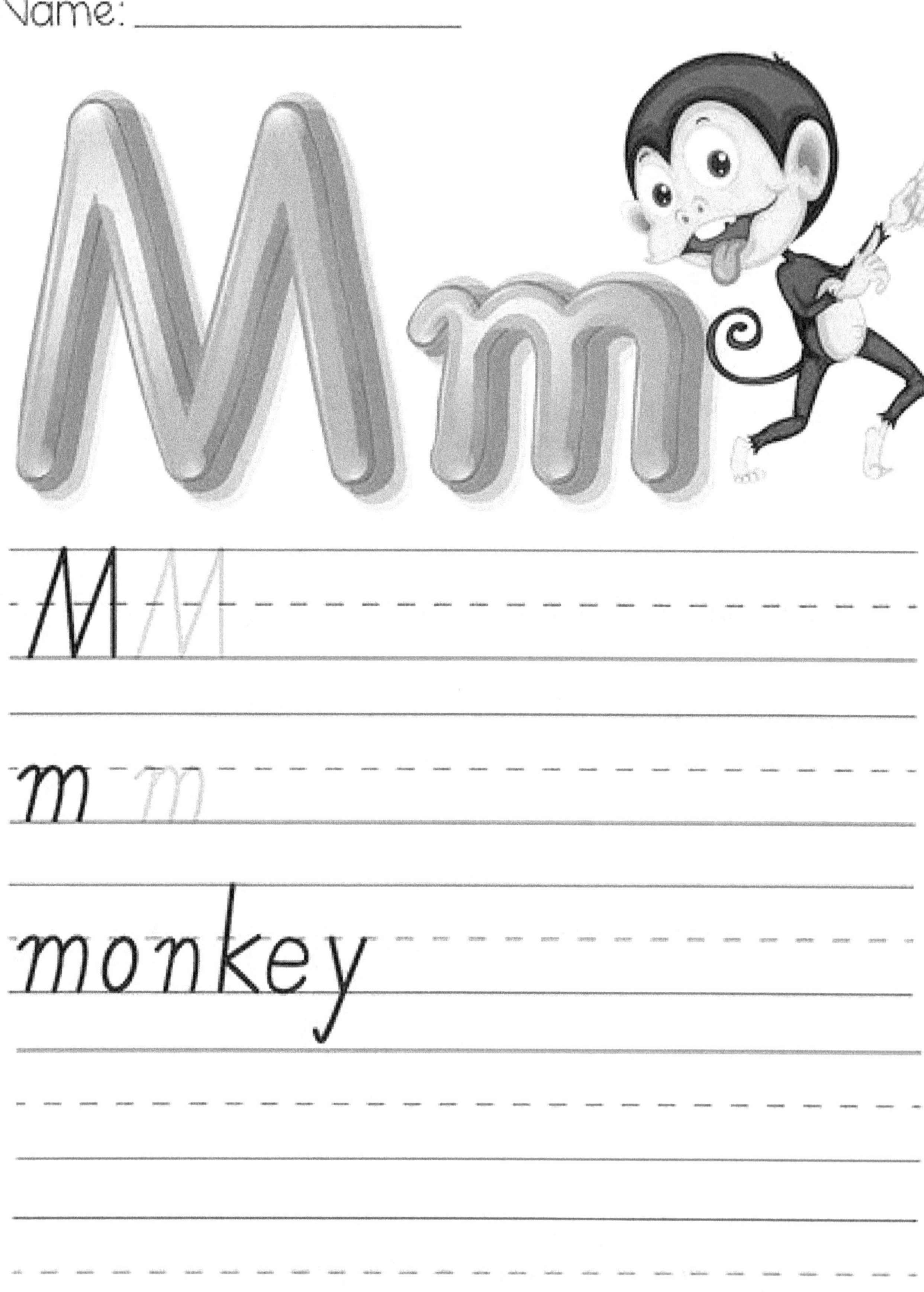

M M

m m

monkey

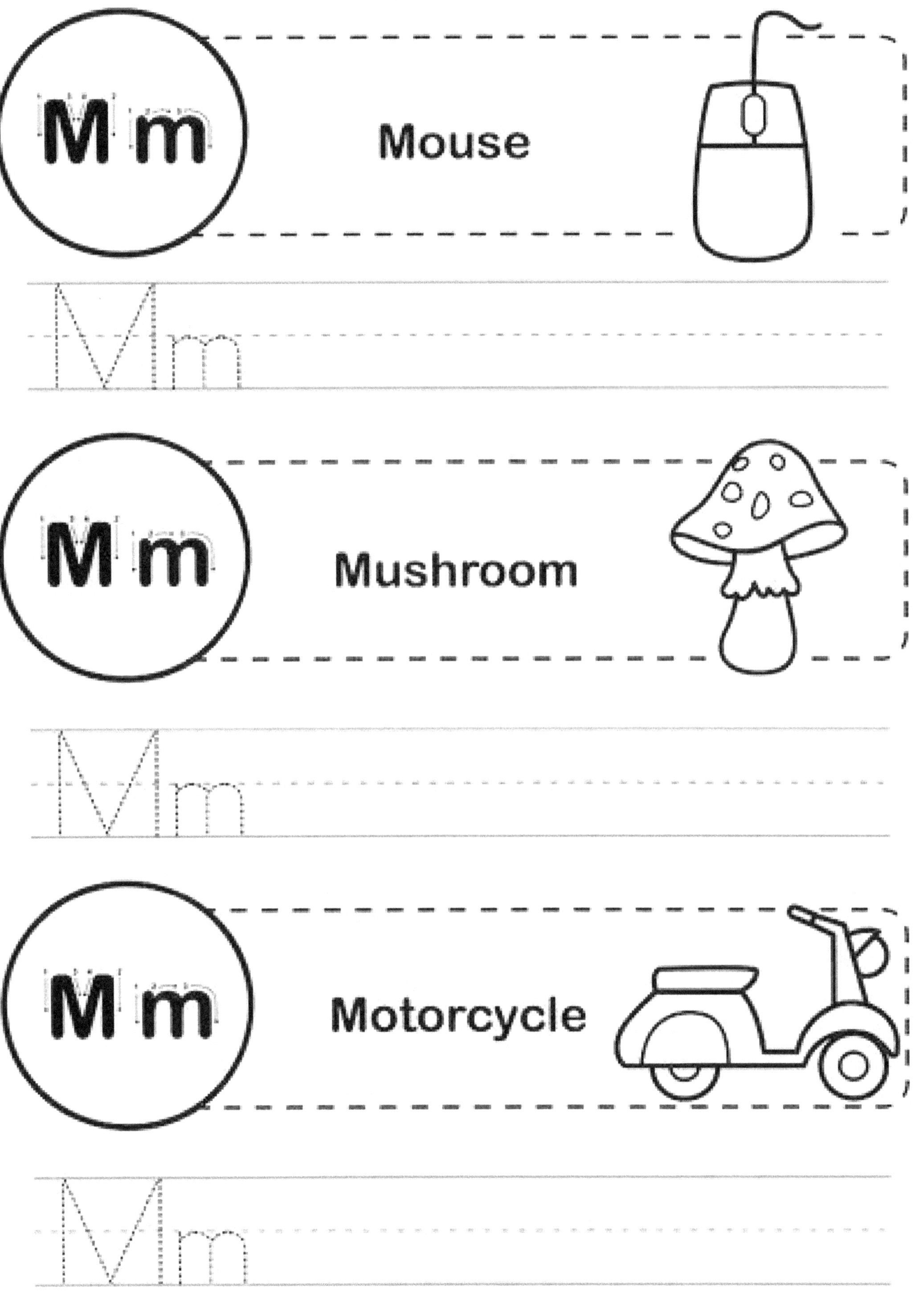

M m Mouse

M m

M m Mushroom

M m

M m Motorcycle

M m

Numbat

N n

N N

n n

nest

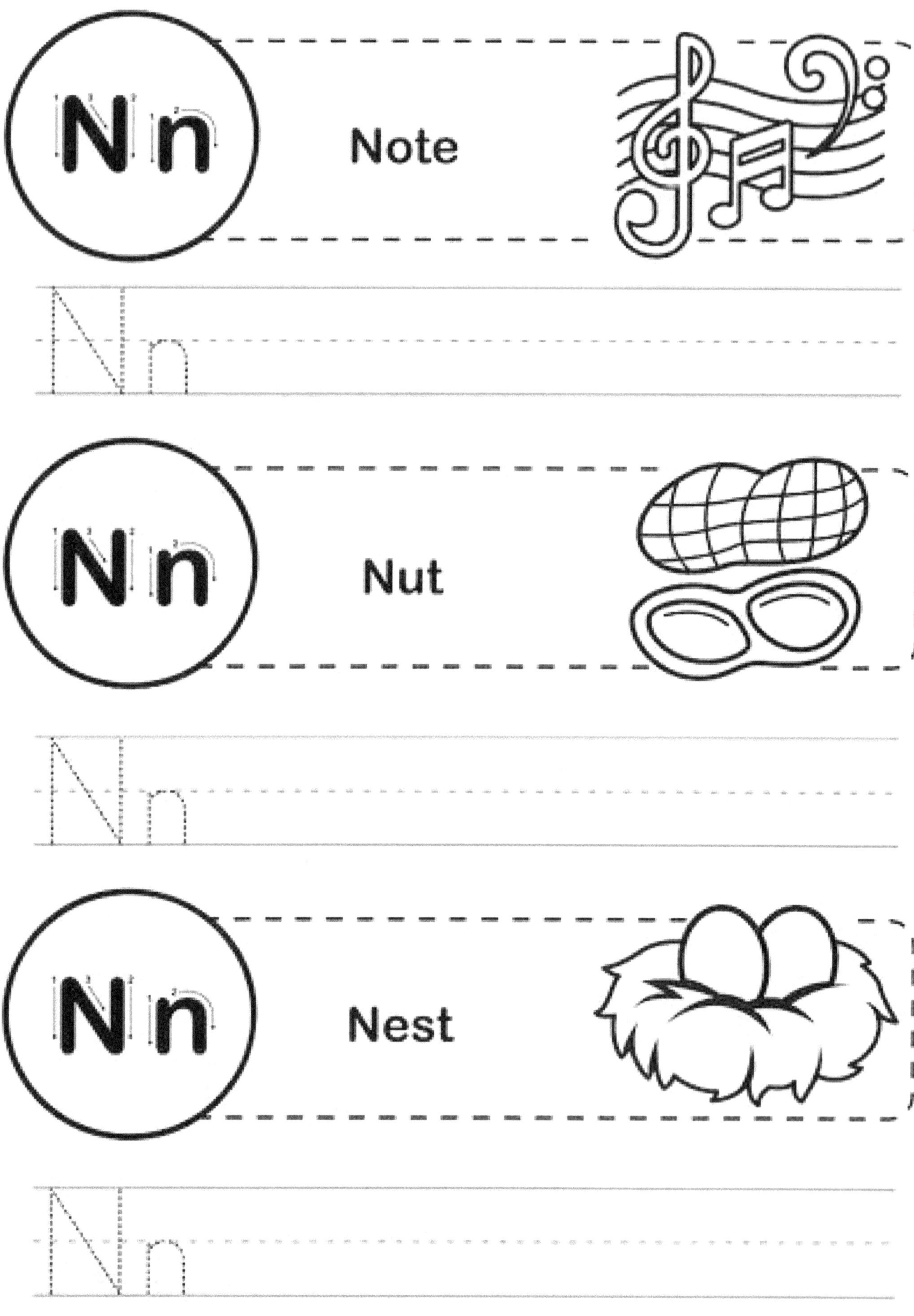

N n
Note
N n
N n
Nut
N n
N n
Nest
N n

Owl

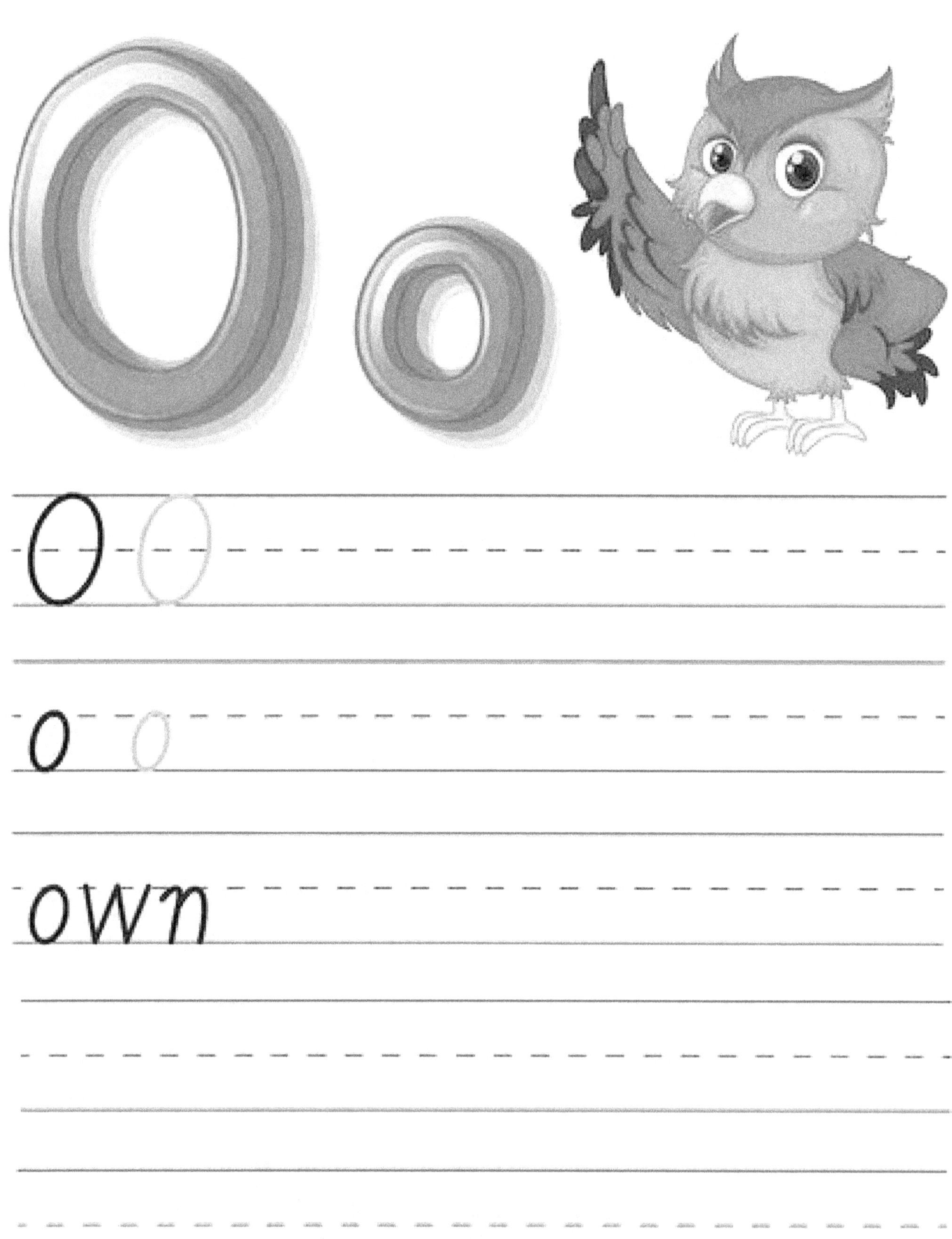

O O

o o

own

Orange
Owl
Old

Penguin

P p

P P

p p

panda

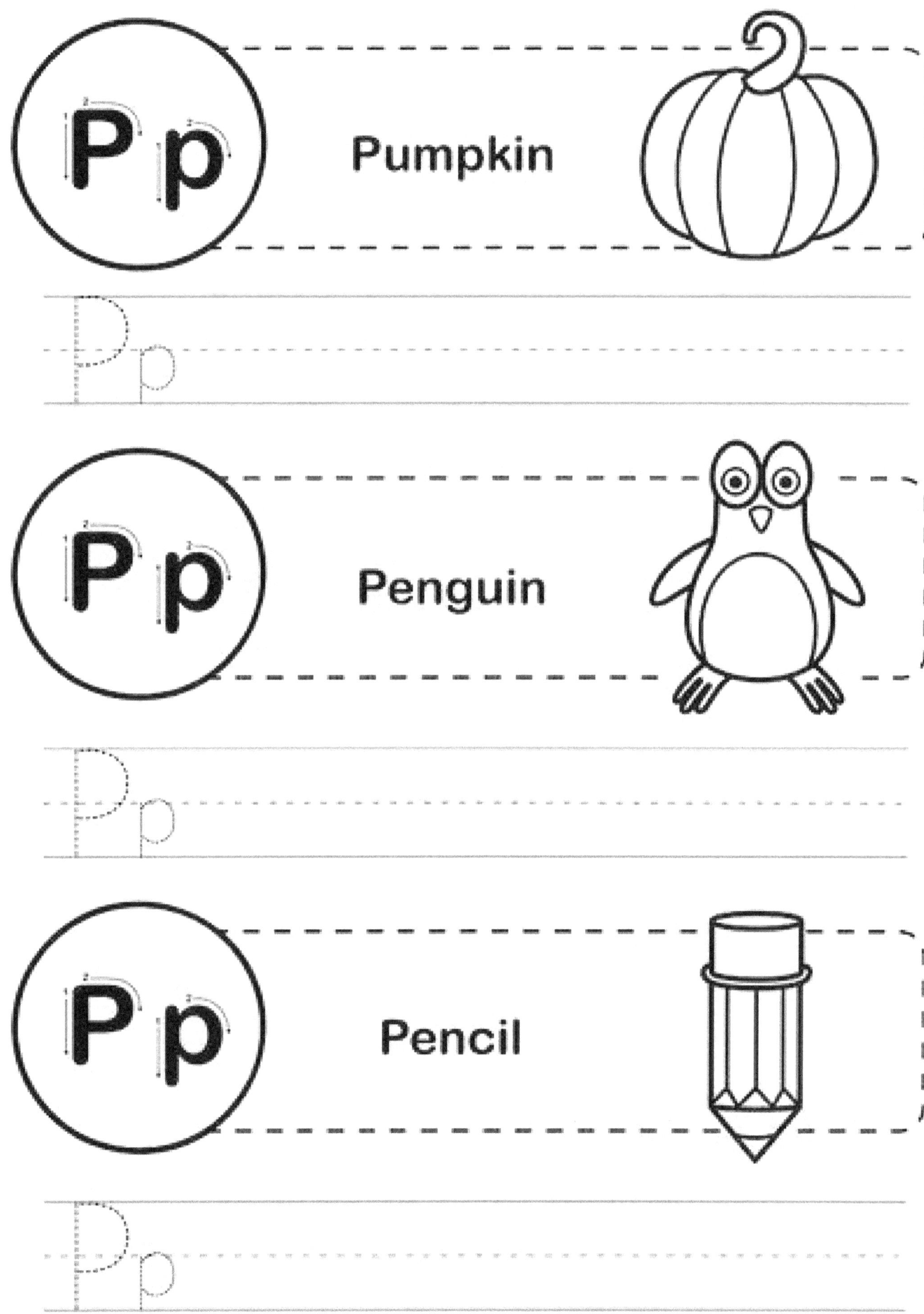

P p
Pumpkin
P p
P p
Penguin
P p
P p
Pencil
P p

Quail

Q Q

q q

quill

Q q
Quail
Q q
Quince
Q q
Quilt

Raccoon

R r

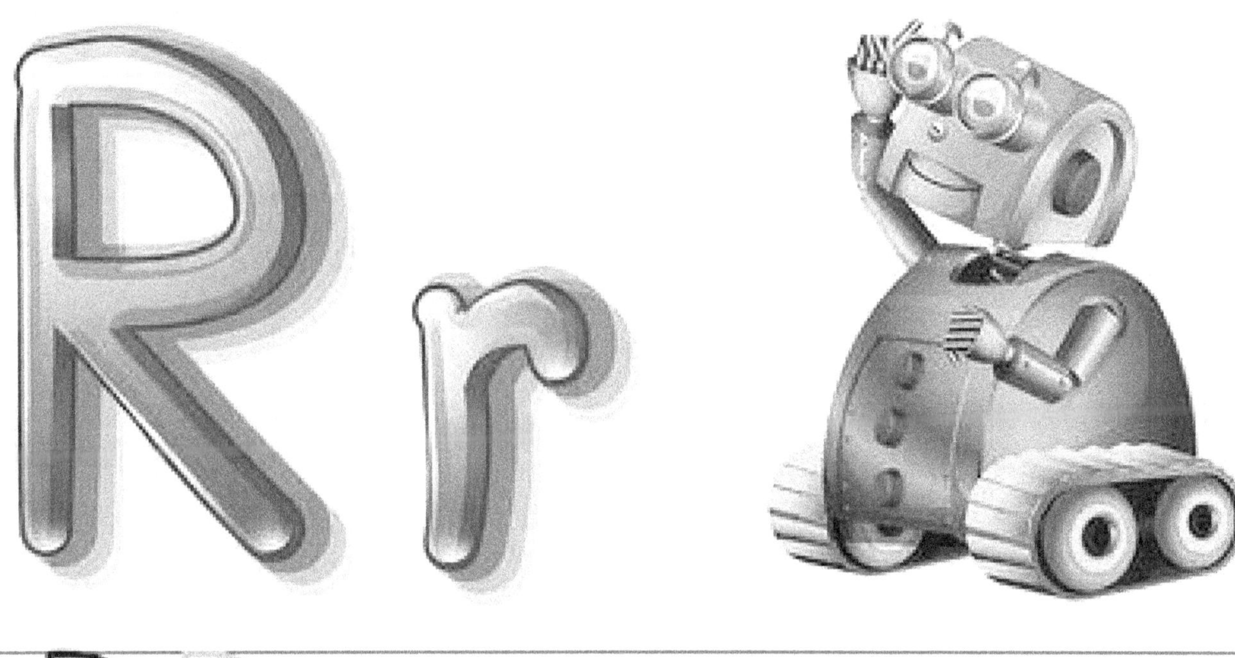

R R

r r

robot

Rocket

Robot

Rabbit

Sheep

S s

S s

s s

snake

S s
Socks
S s
Sheep
S s
Seal

Turtle

Name:

T
t
toilet

T t

Tomato

T t

Telephone

T t

Turtle

Unicorn

U U

u u

umbrella

U u
Ufo
U u
Unicorn
U u
Umbrella

Vampire

Name:

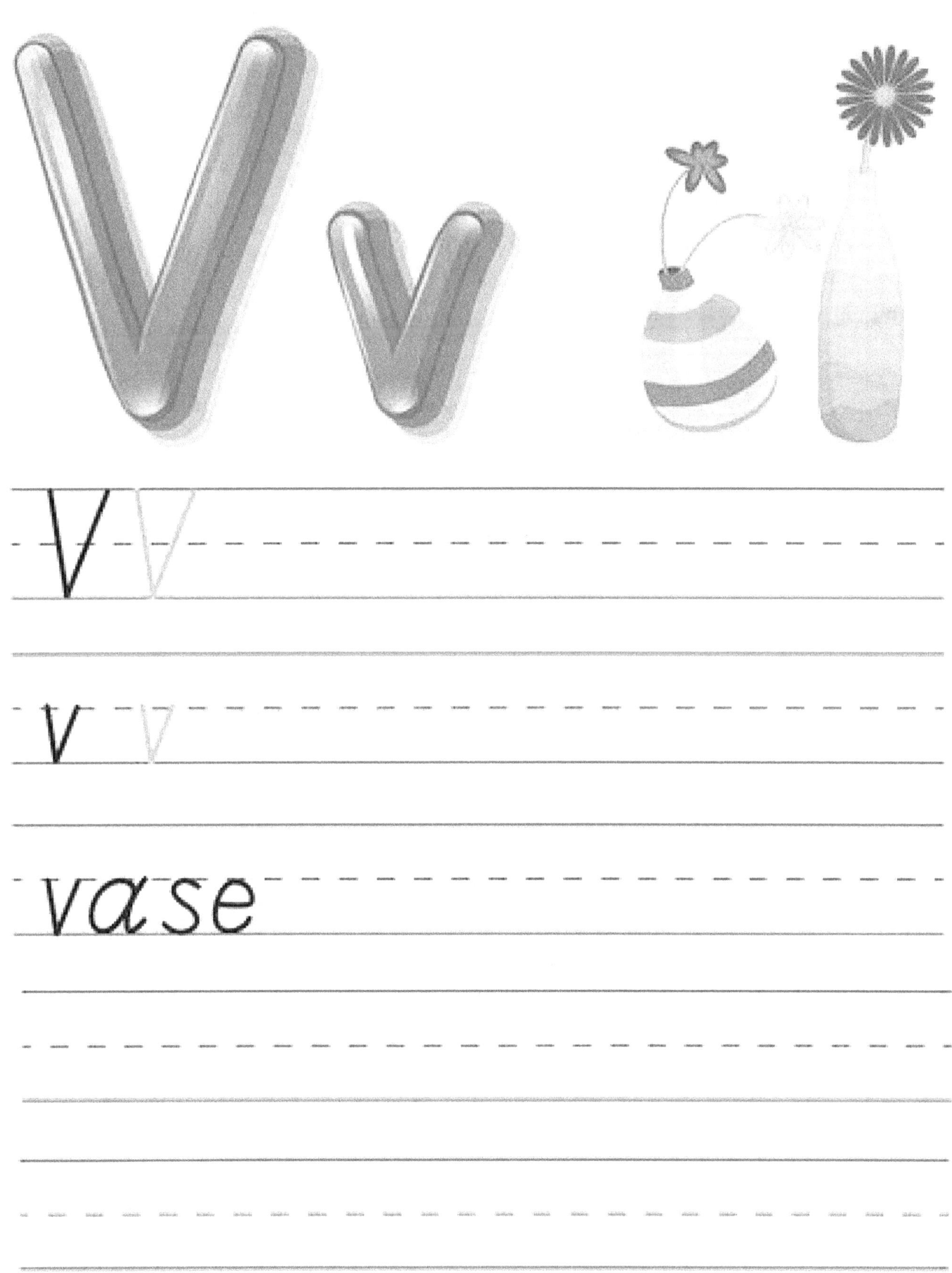
V v
V
v
vase

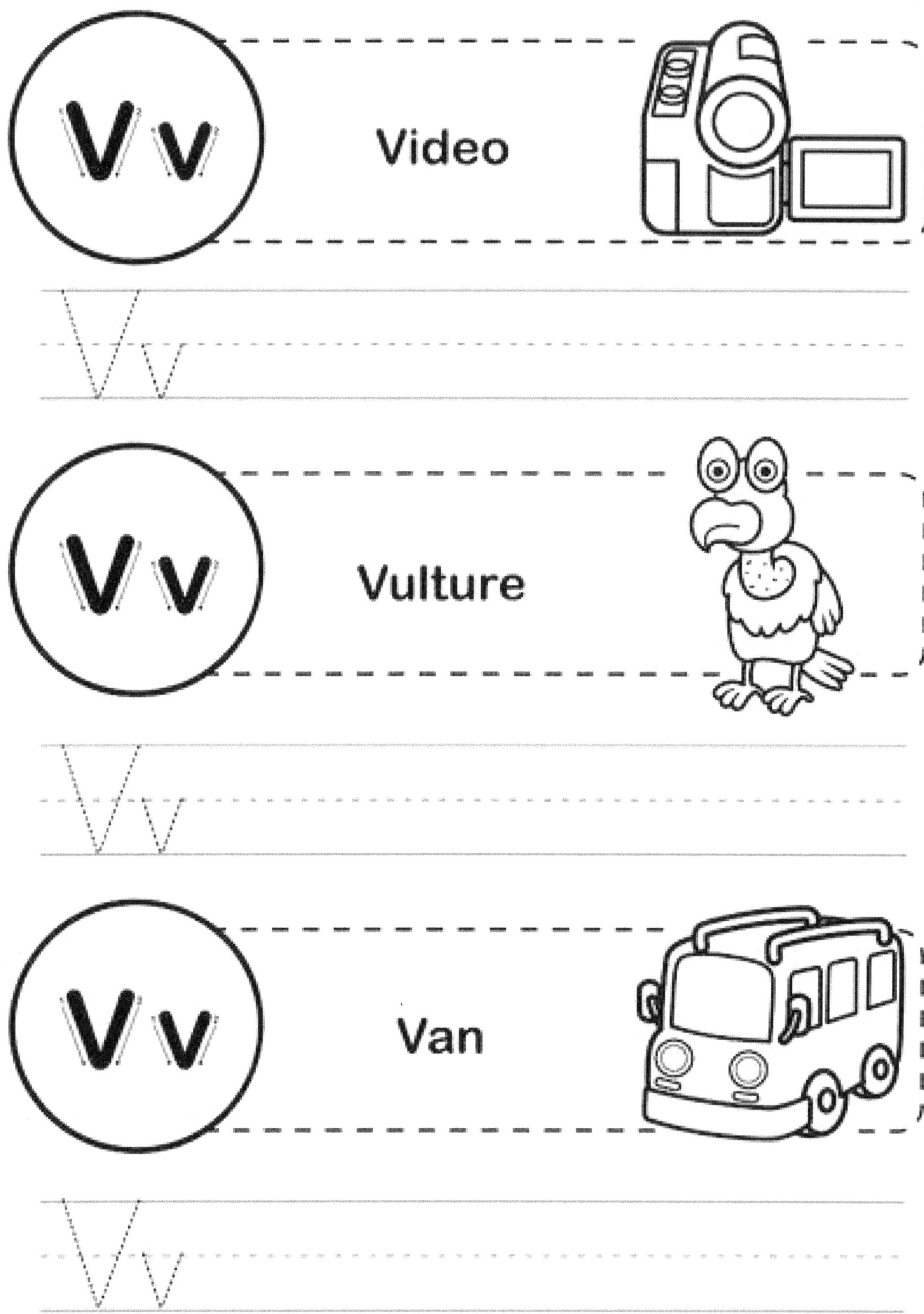
Vv
Video
Vv
Vulture
Vv
Van

Whale

W W

w w

well

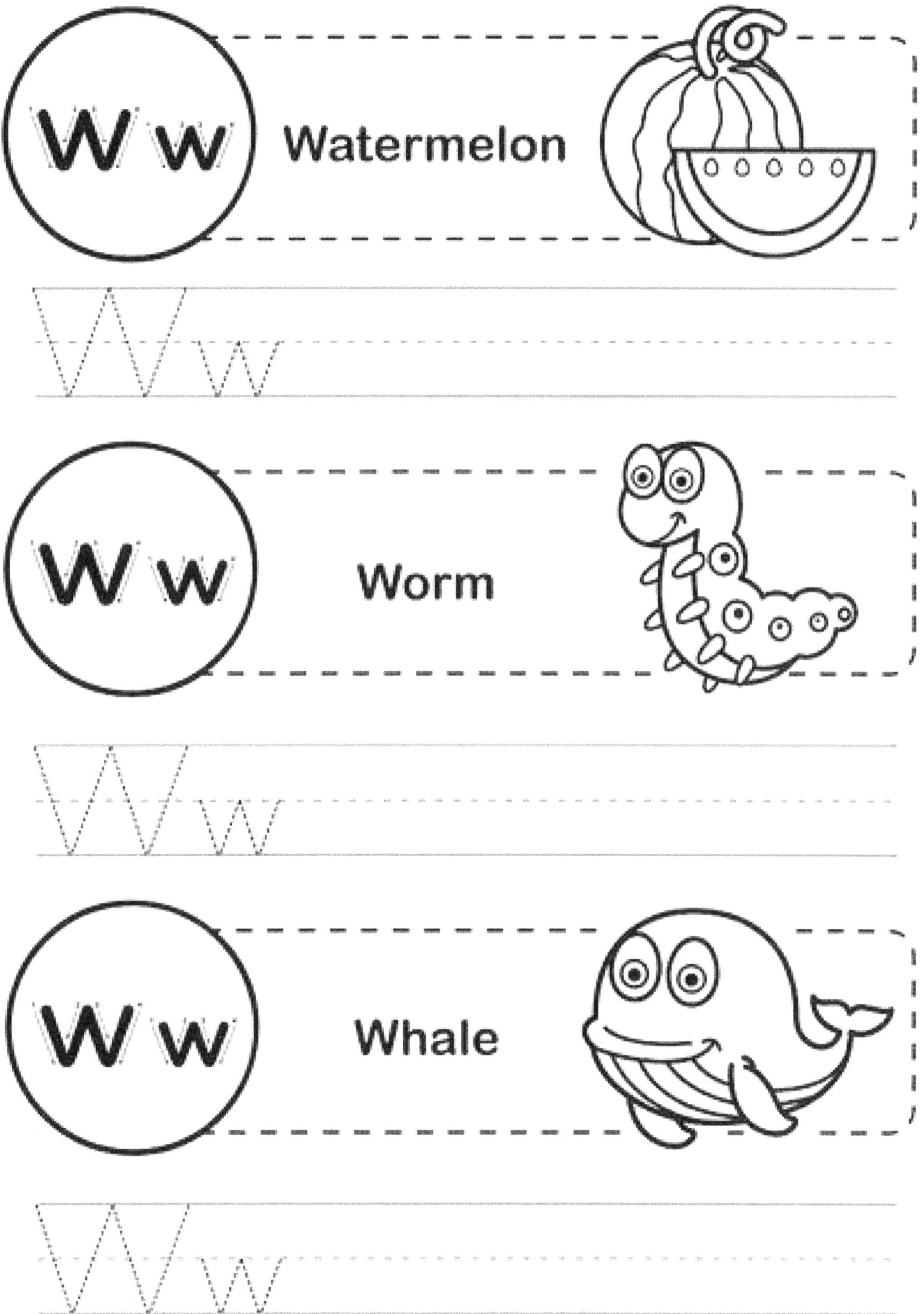

Watermelon

Worm

Whale

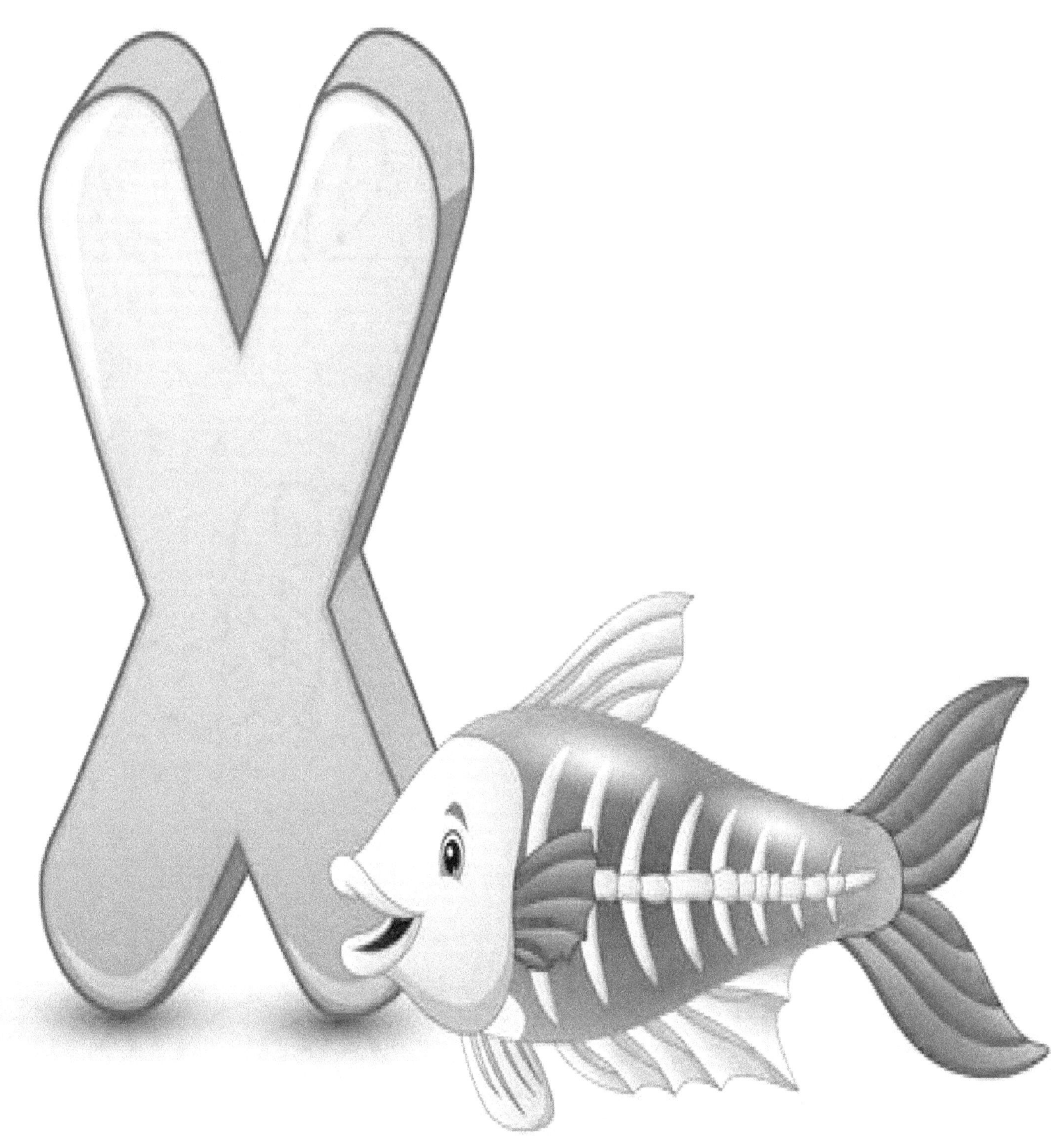

X-ray Fish

Name: ___________________

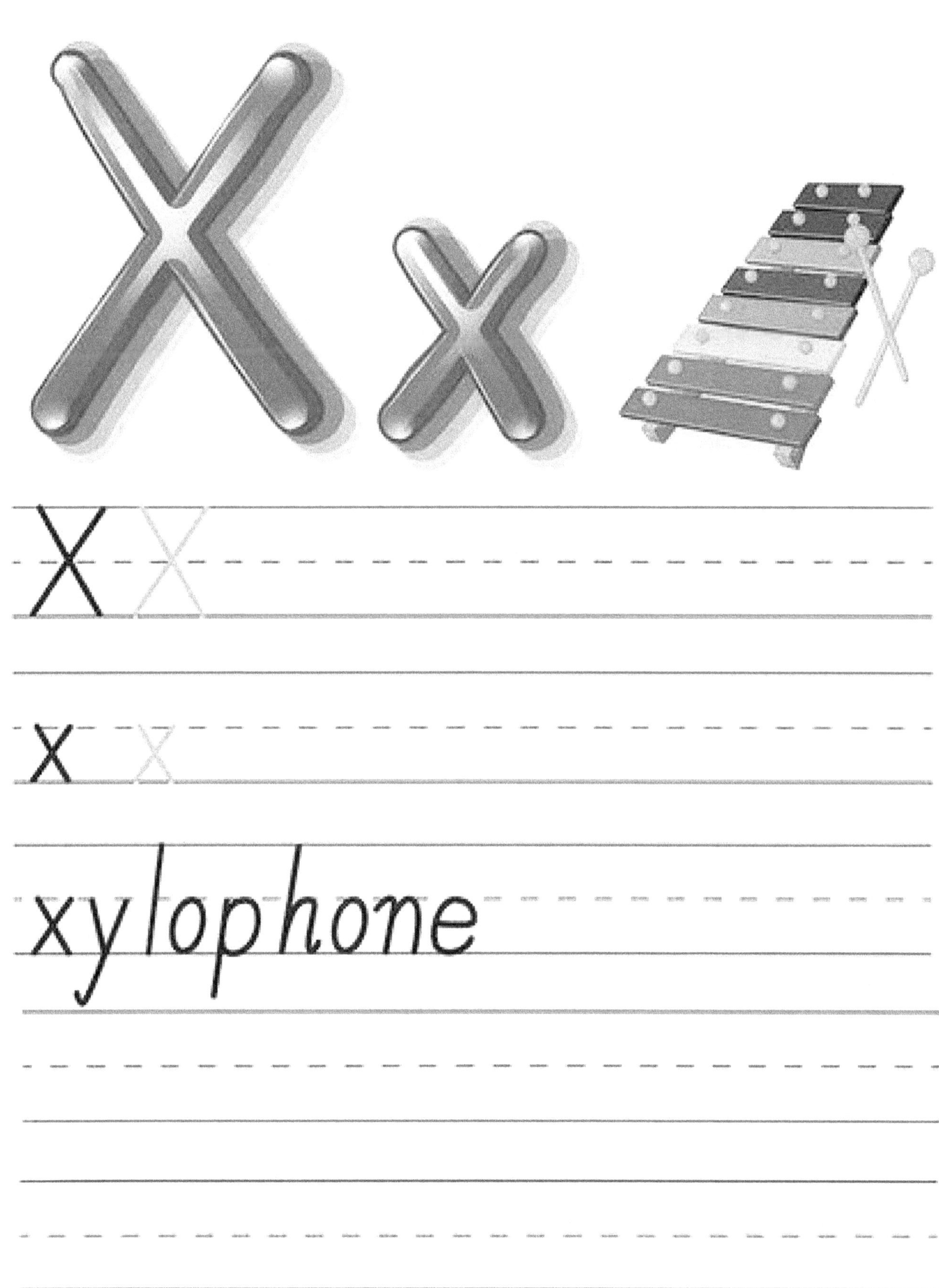

X x
X X
x x
xylophone

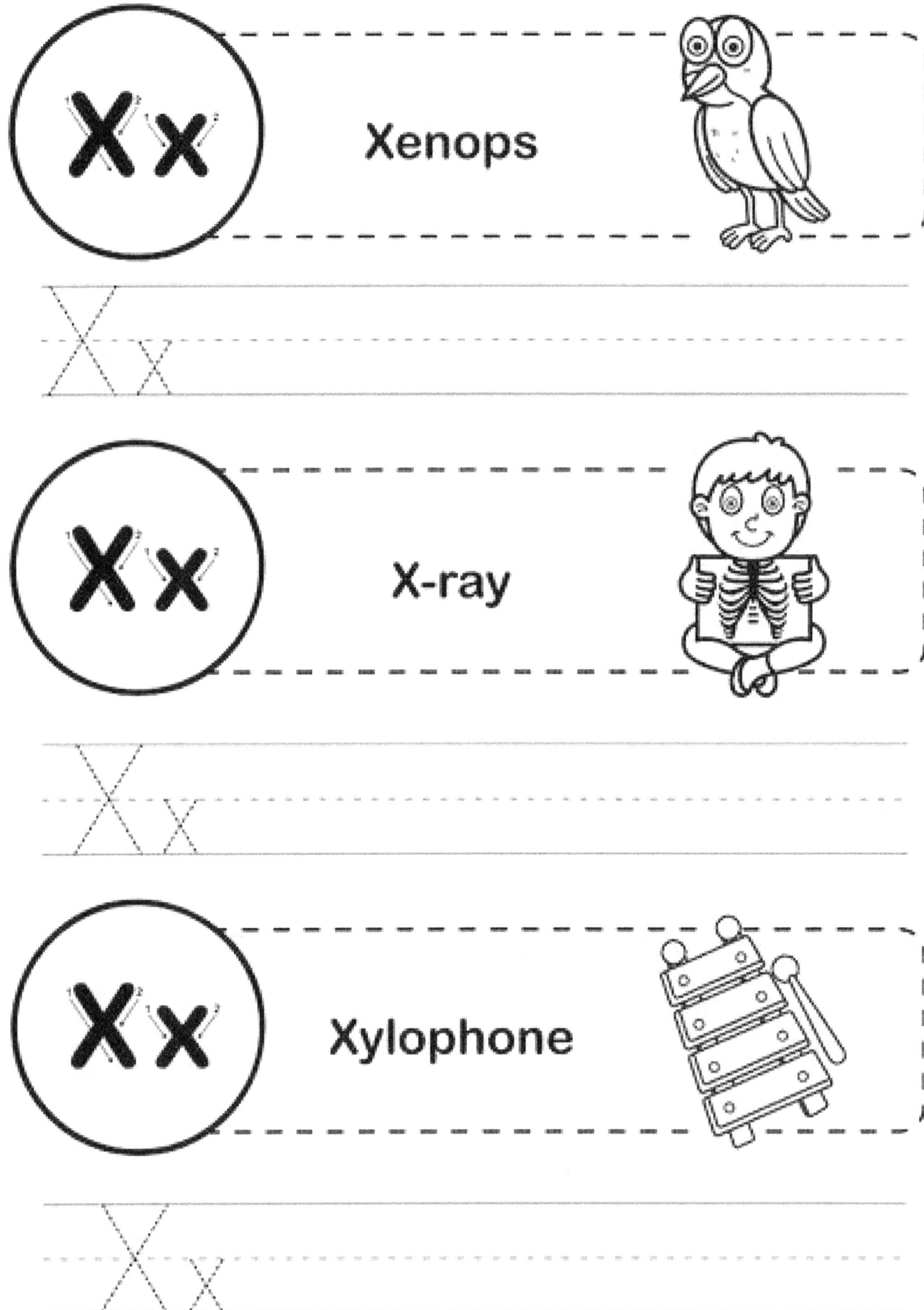

Xenops

X-ray

Xylophone

Yak

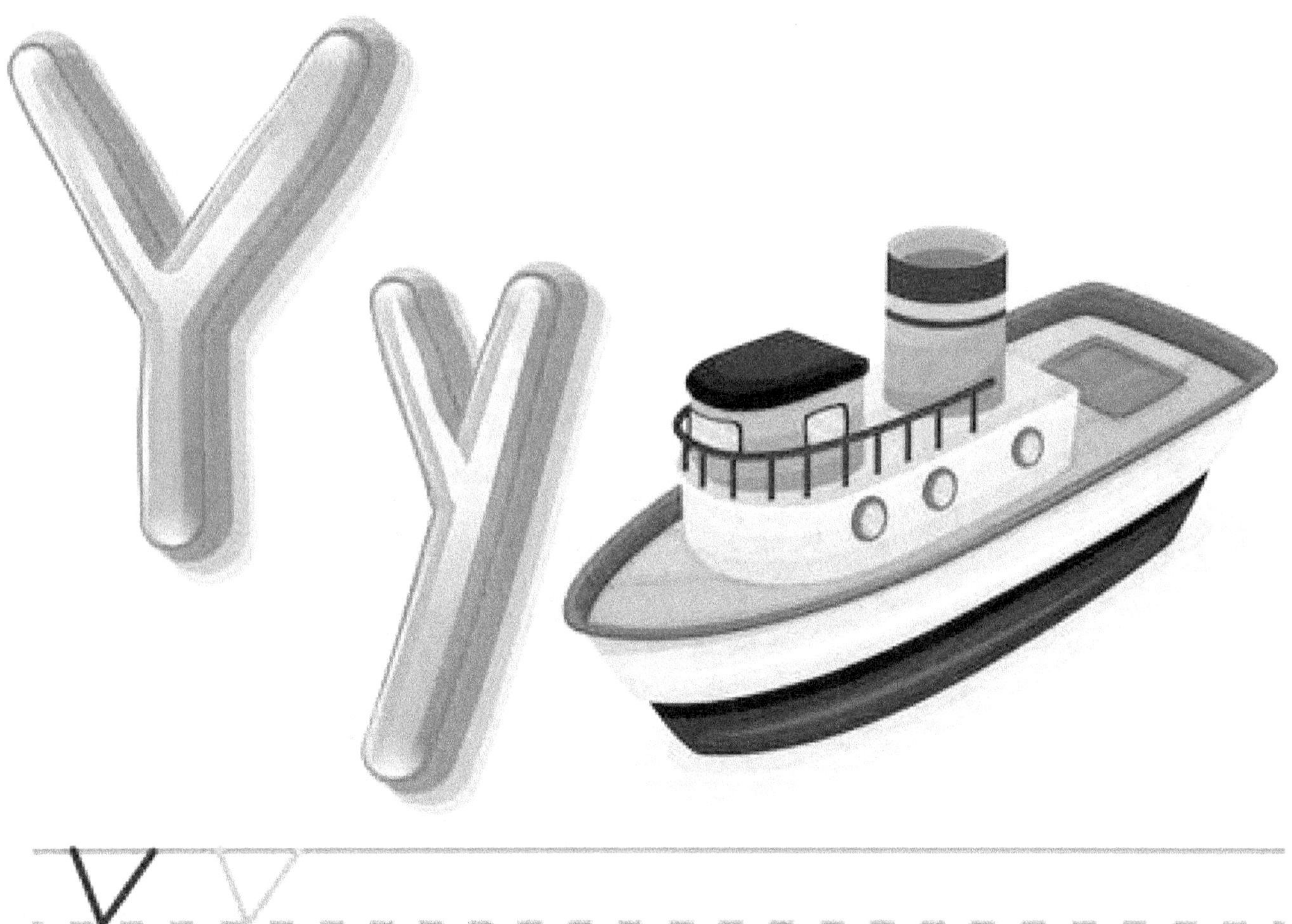

Y Y

y y

yacht

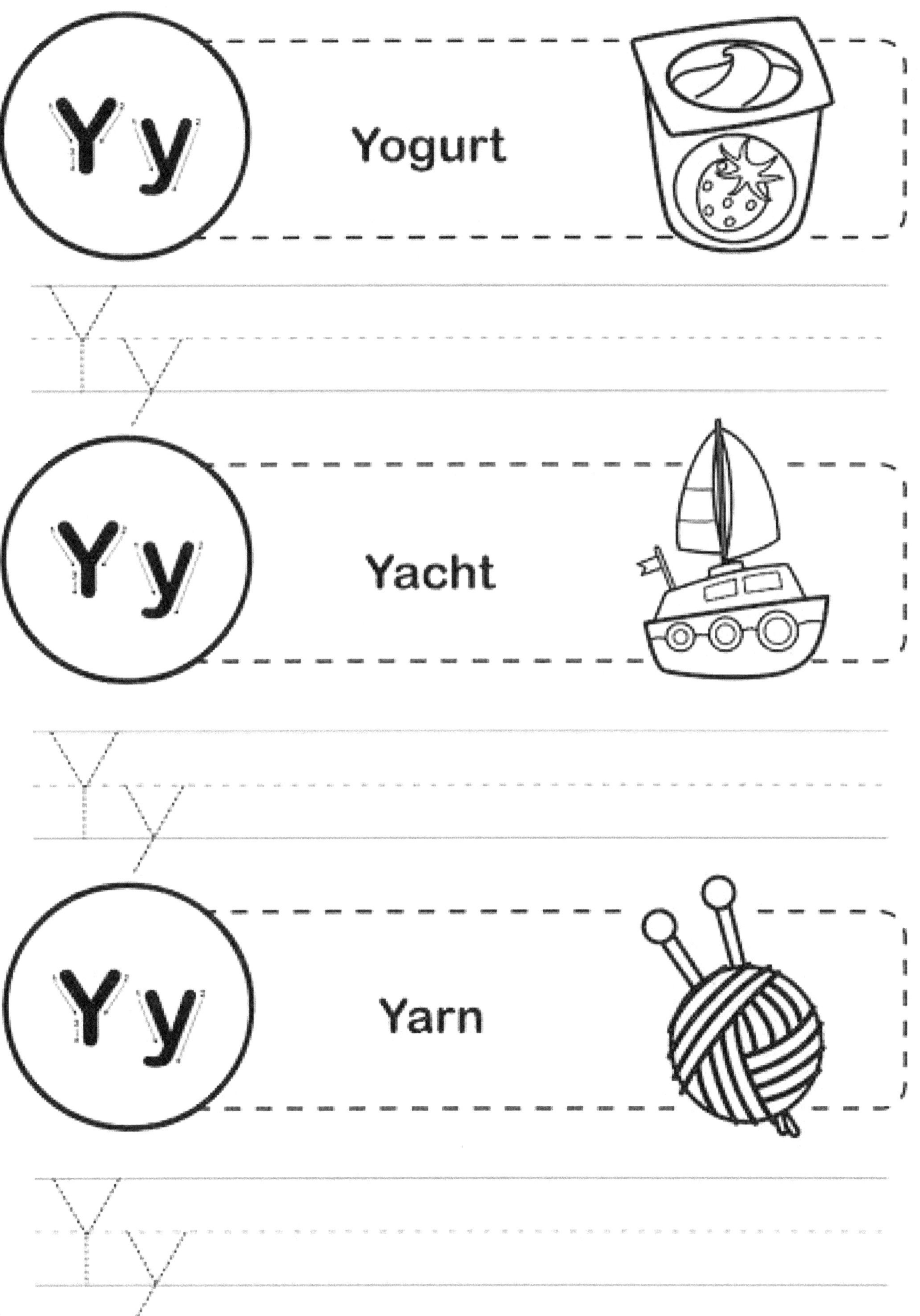

Yogurt

Yacht

Yarn

Zebra

Name: ________________

Z z
z
z
zebra

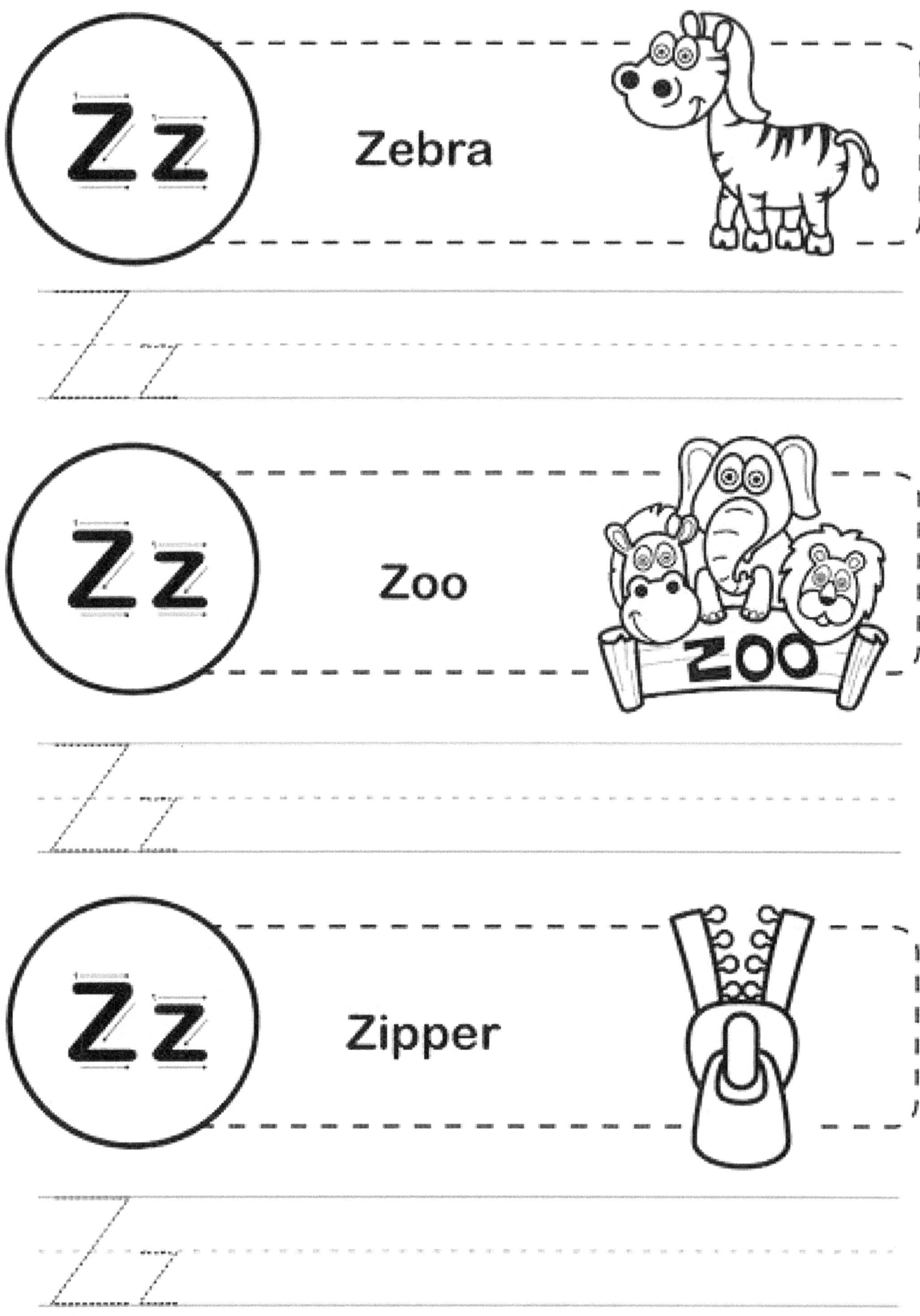

Z z
Zebra
Z z
Zoo
ZOO
Z z
Zipper

zero

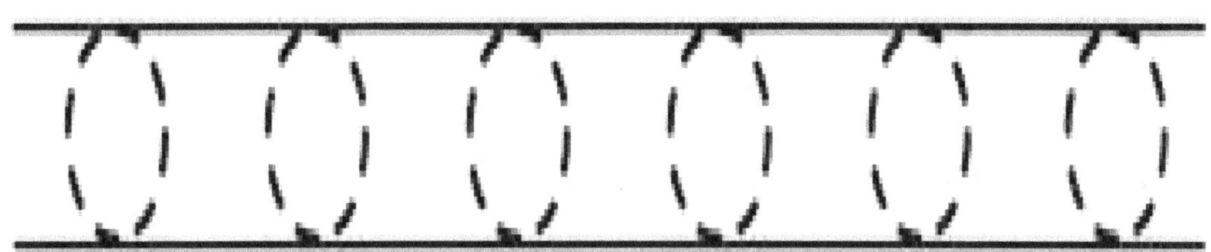

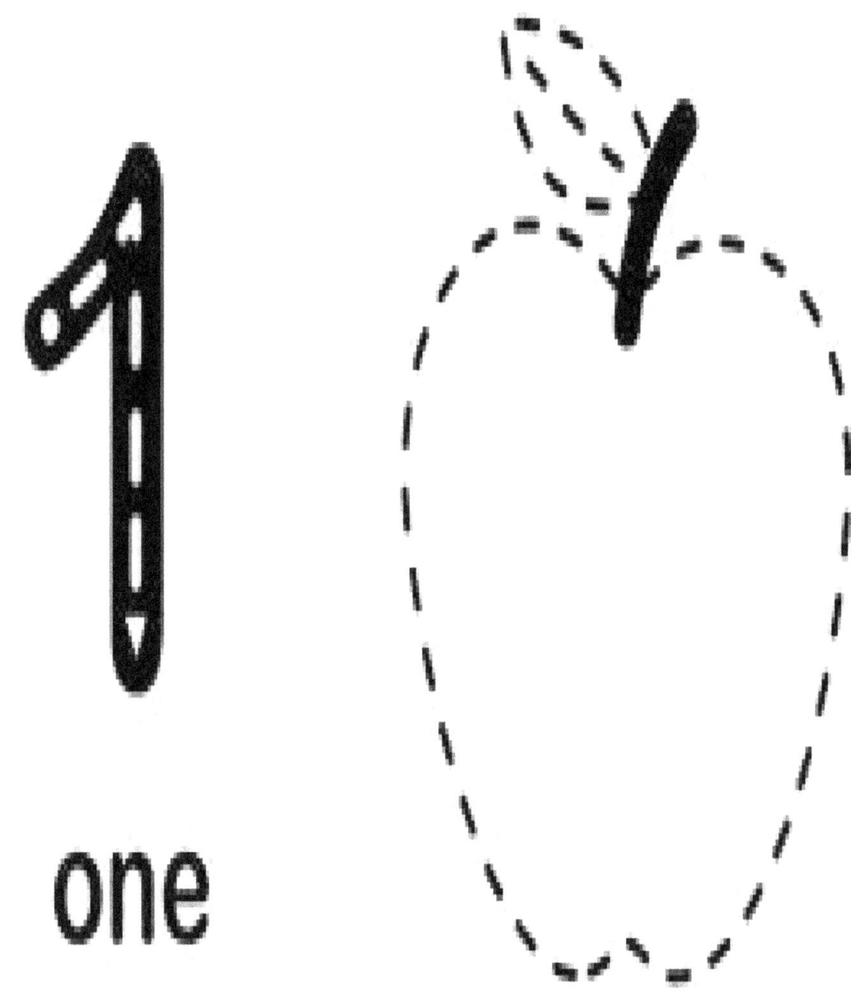

one

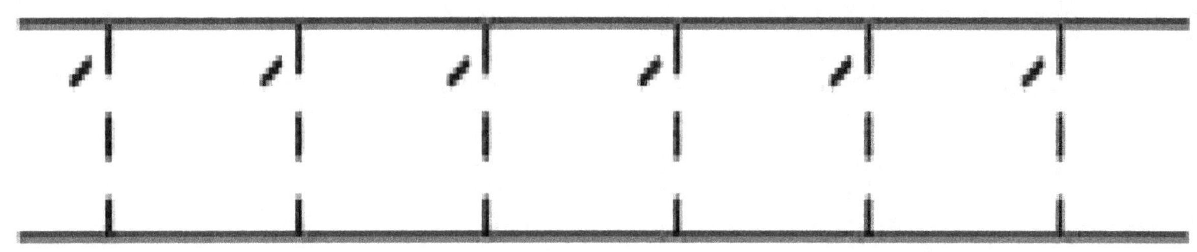

2

two

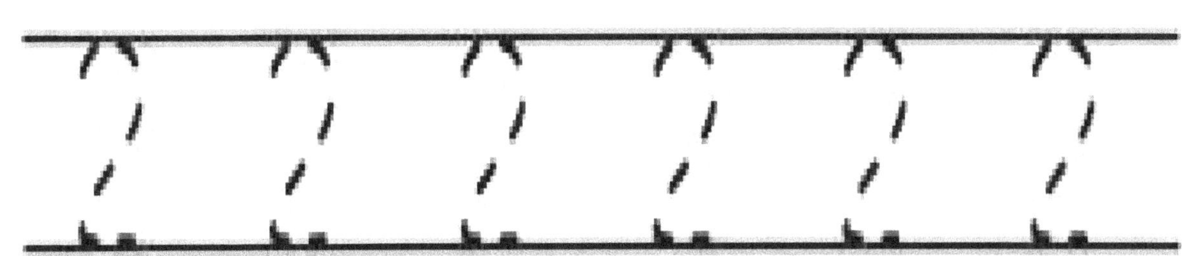

3

three

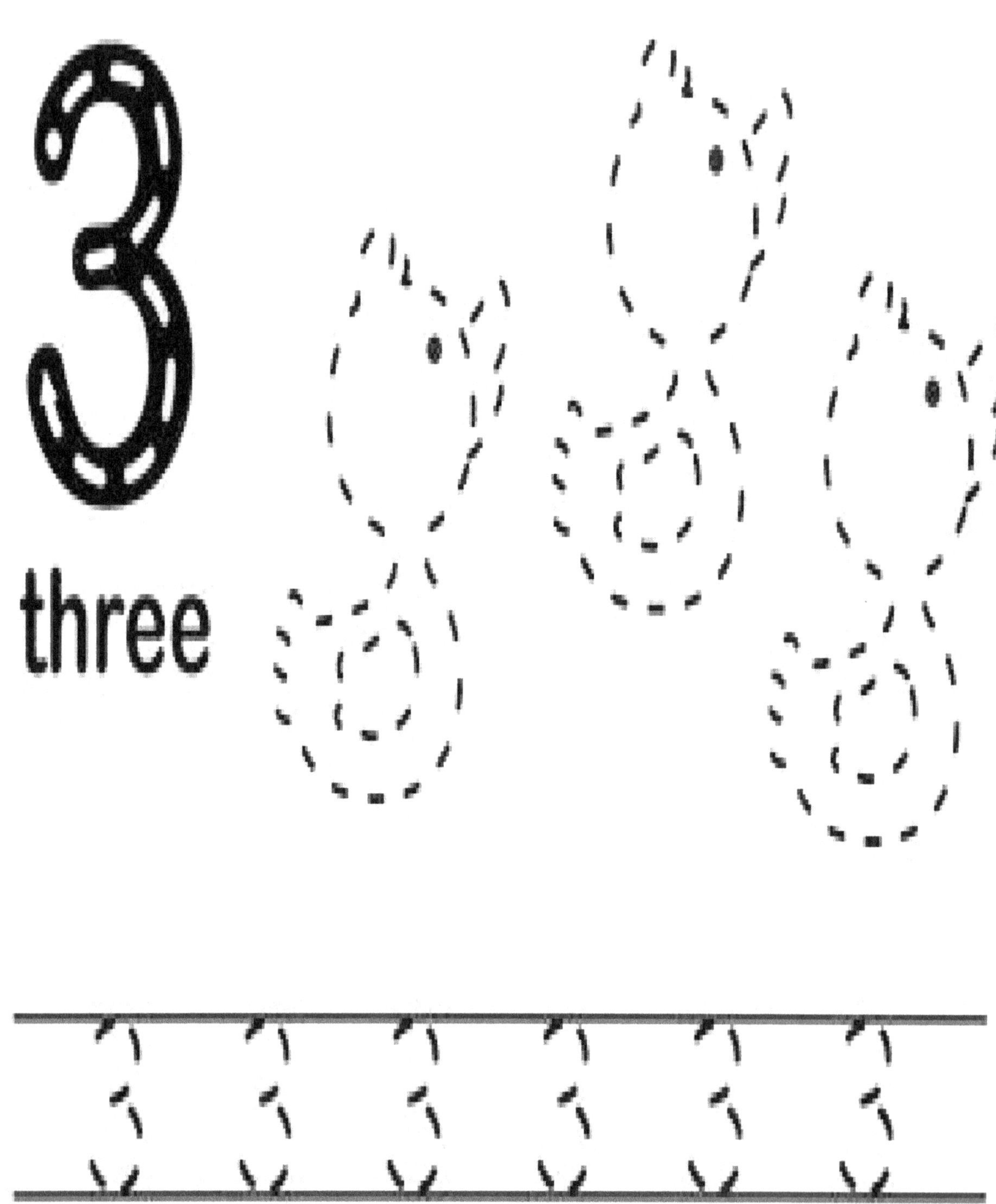

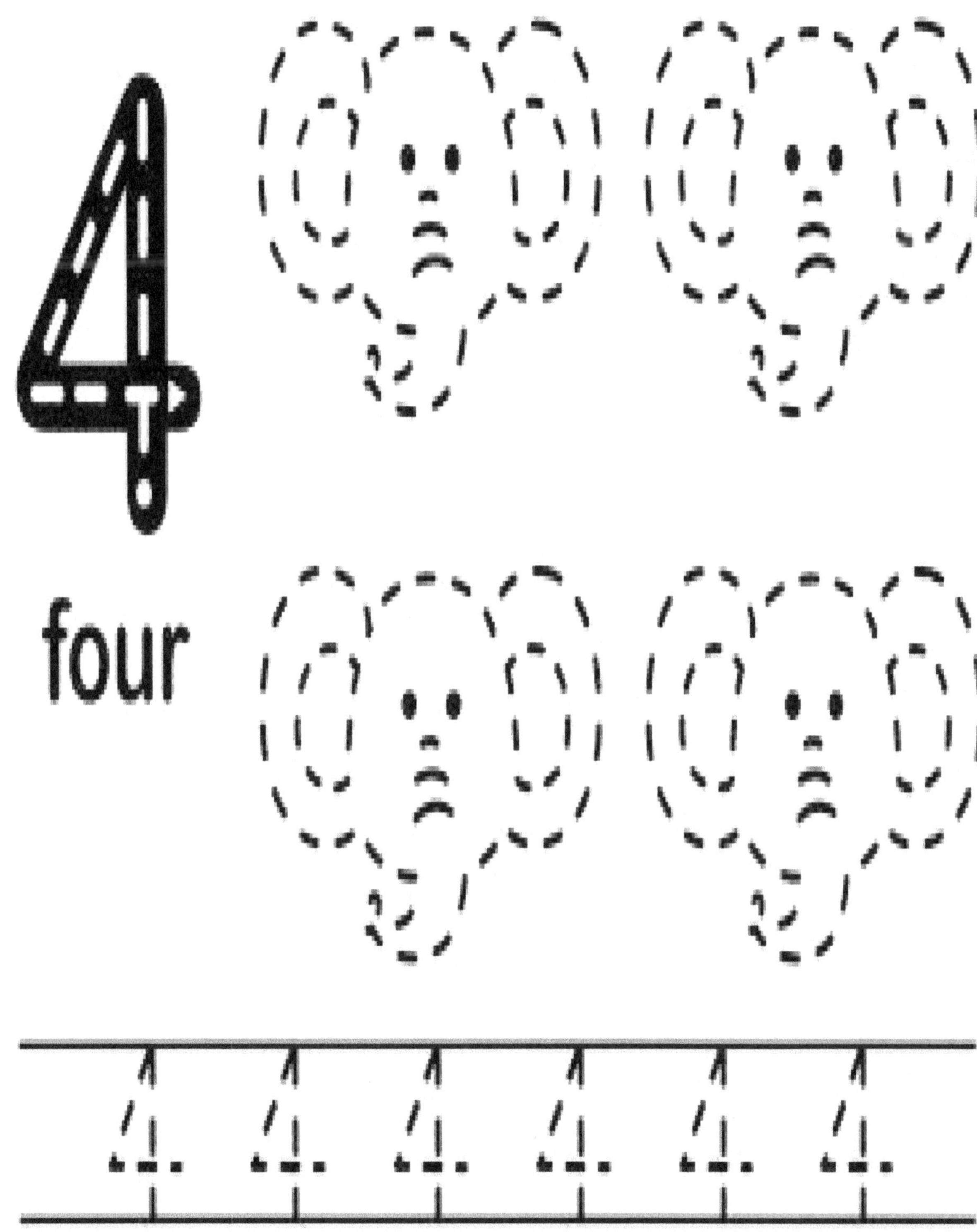

4

four

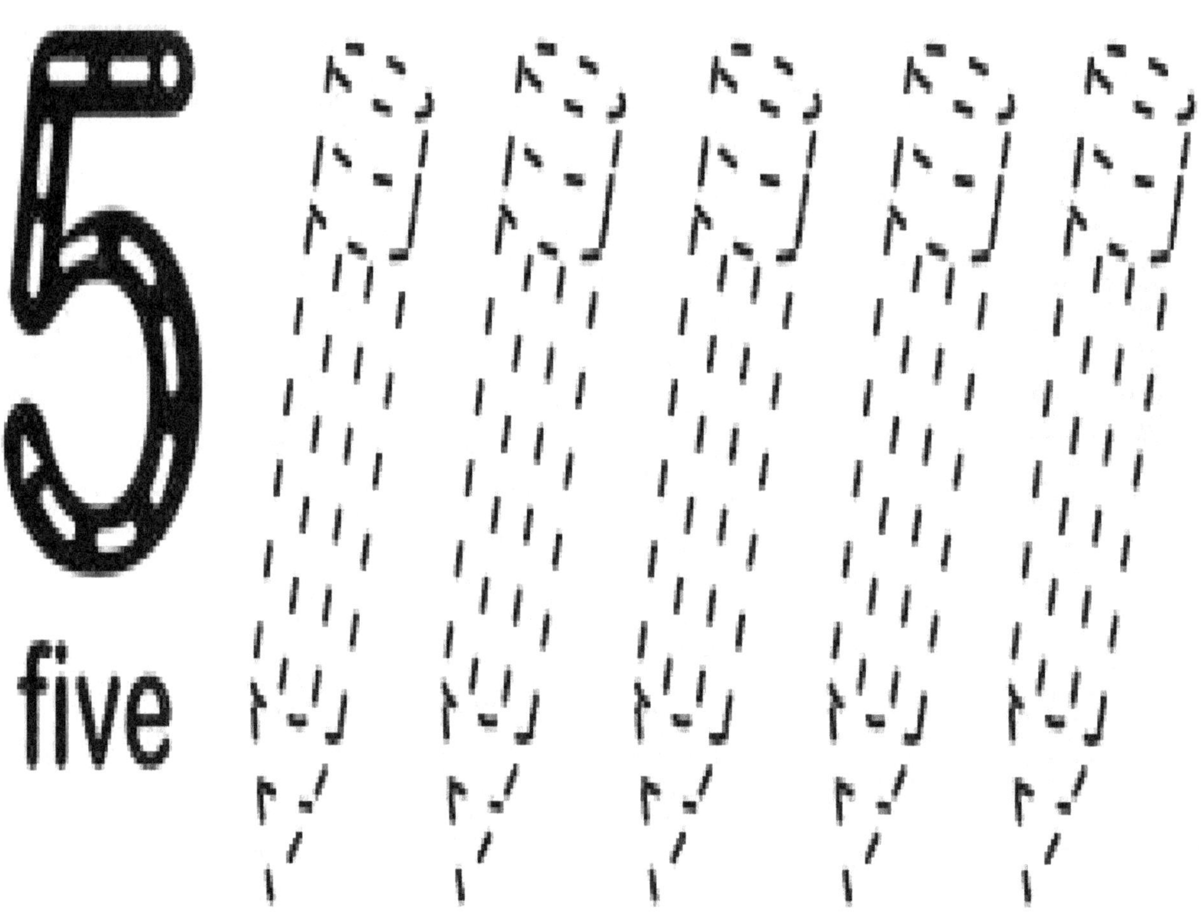

number exercise

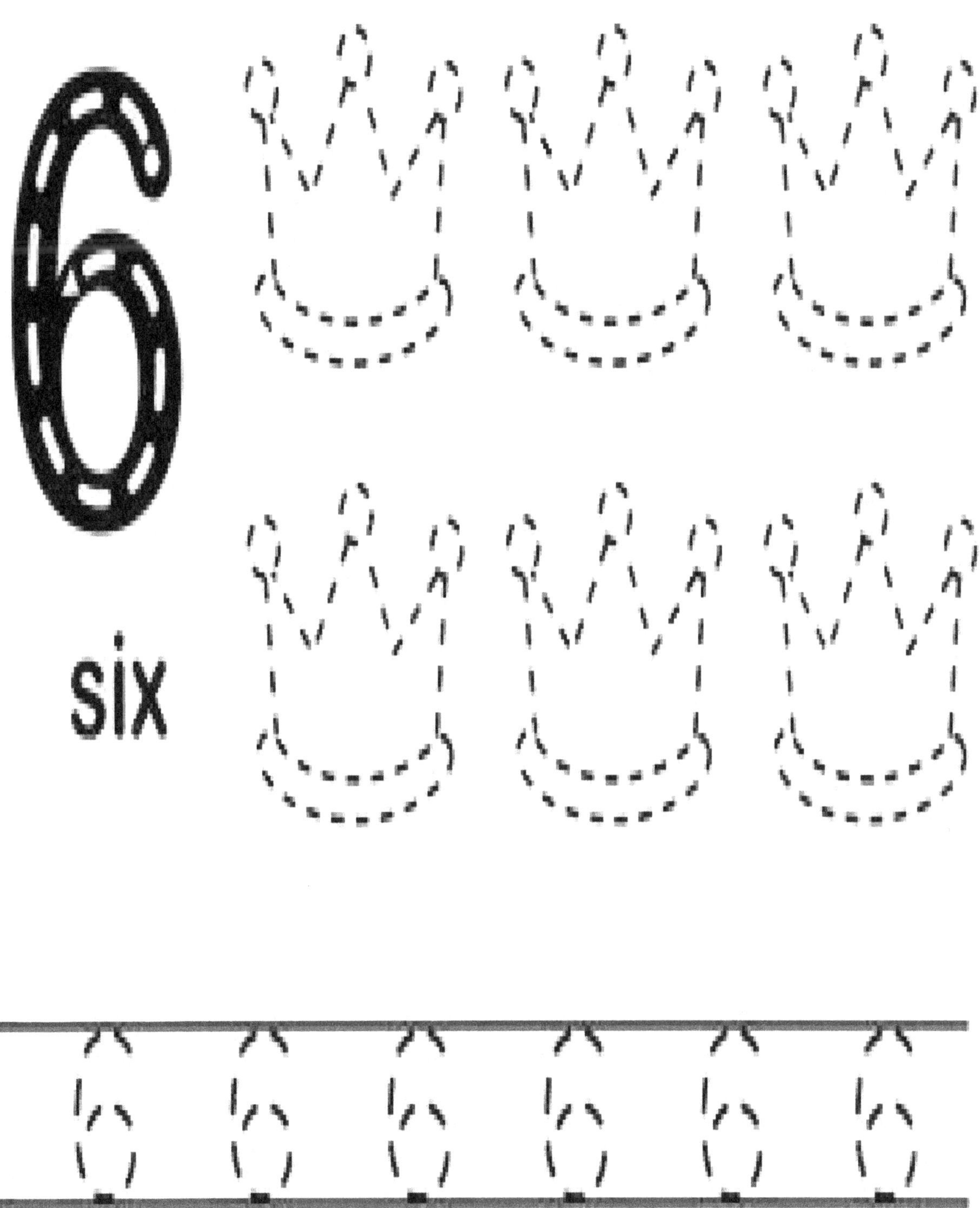

six

number exercise

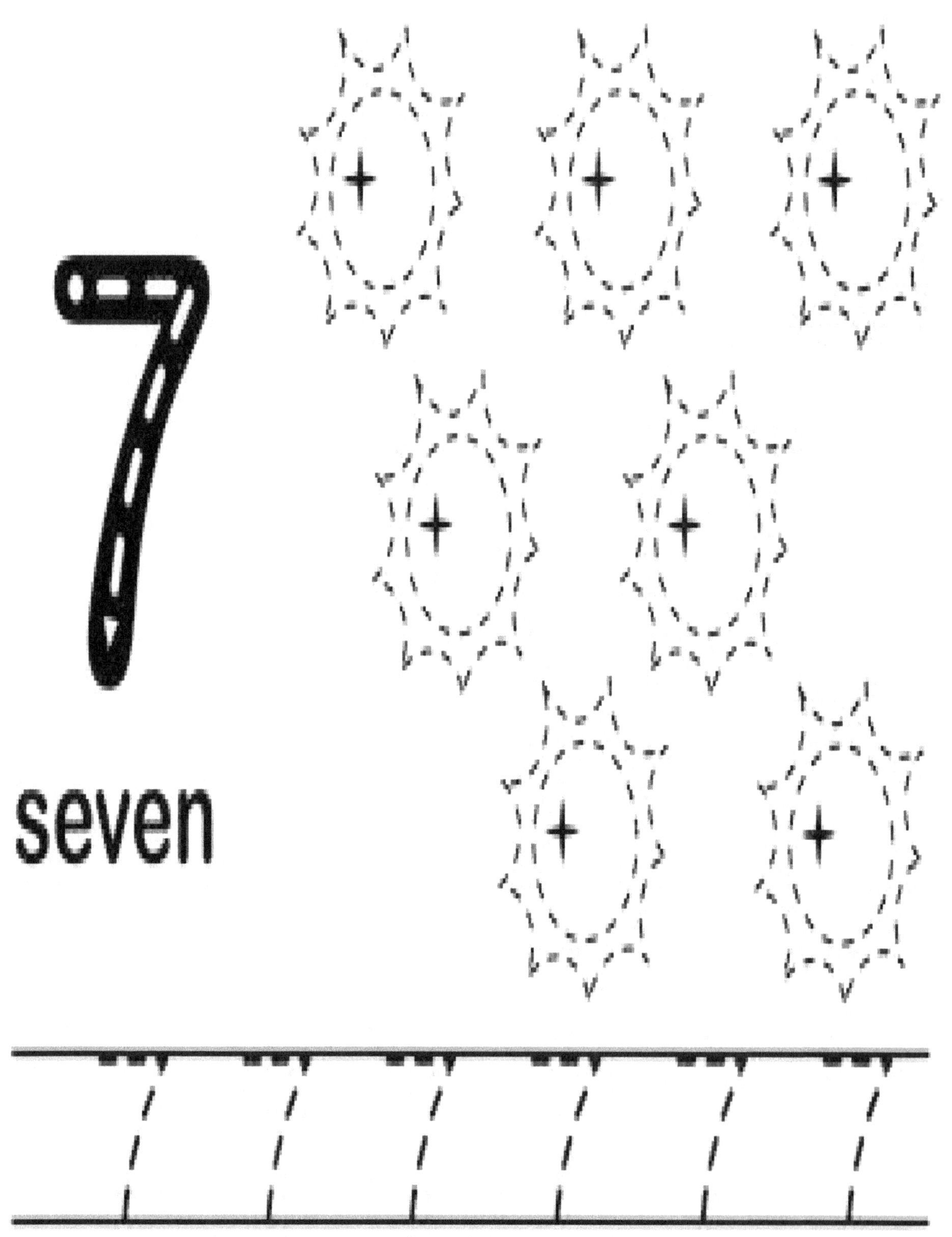

7

seven

number exercise

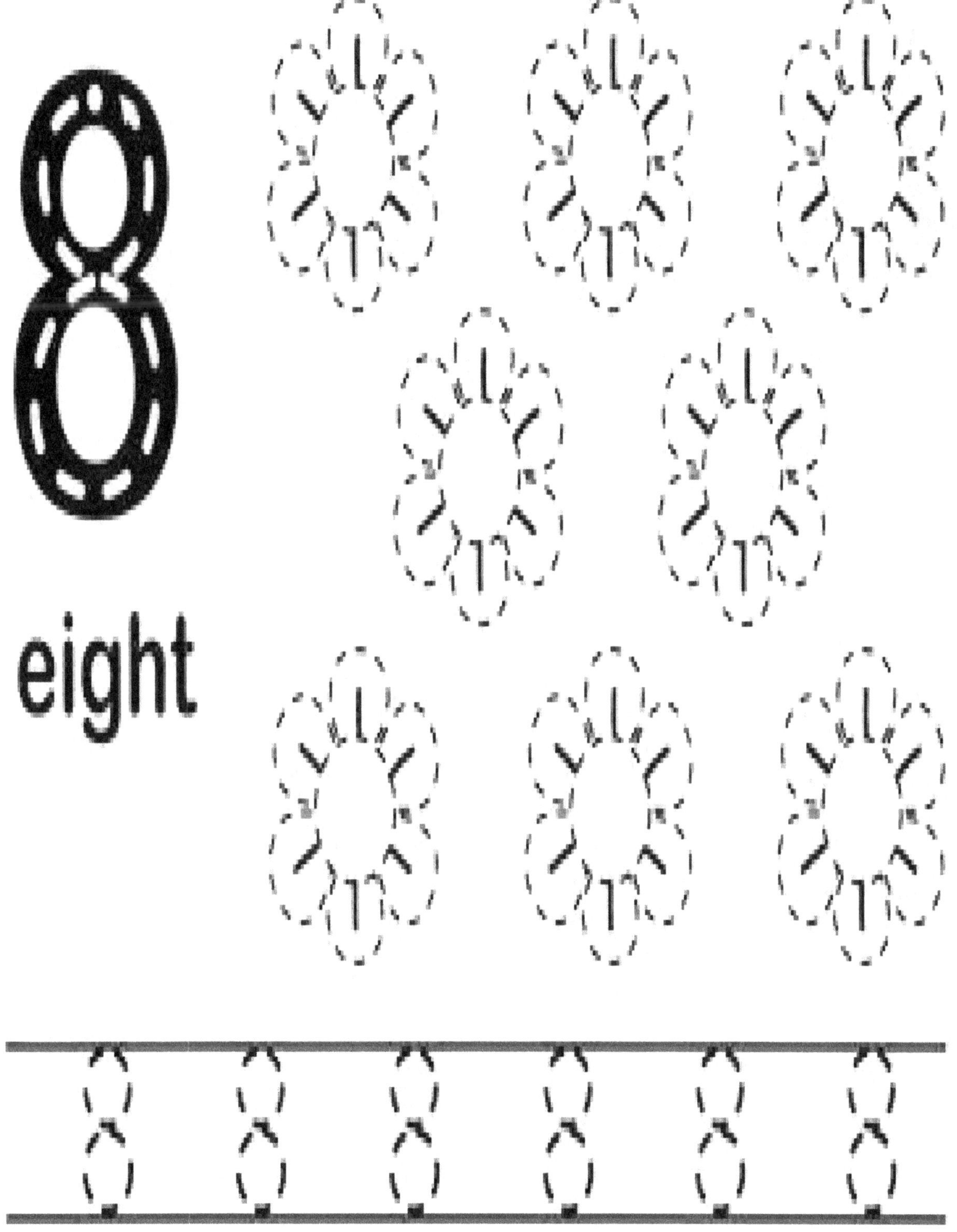

8

eight

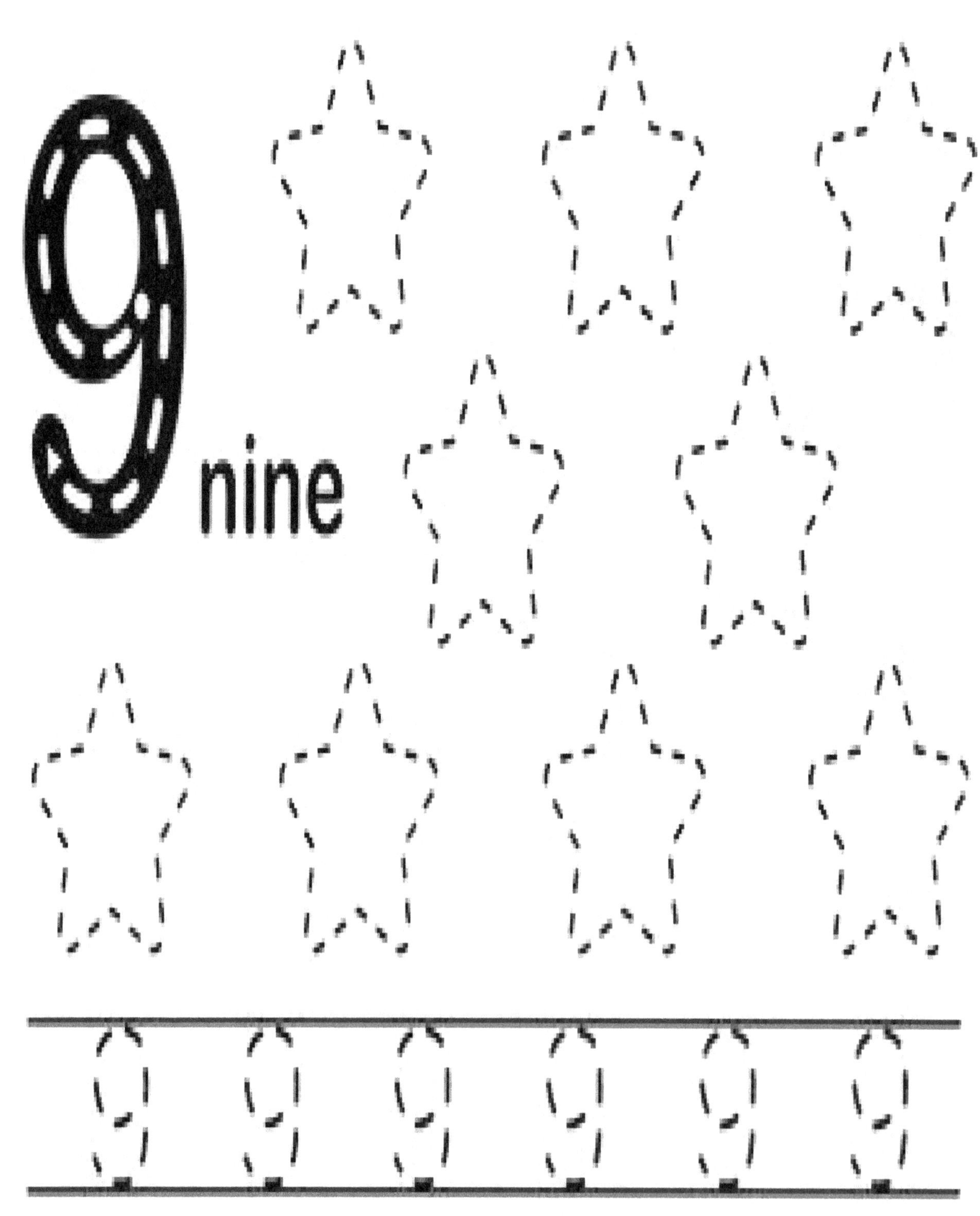

9
nine